GEN Z

The Culture, Beliefs
and Motivations Shaping the
Next Generation

A Barna Report Produced in
Partnership with Impact 360 Institute

Contents

PREFACE

By Jonathan Morrow, Author of Welcome to College *and*
Director of Cultural Engagement, Impact 360 Institute

Is Gen Z prepared to follow Jesus in a post-everything world?

As Christian leaders, pastors, educators and parents, we want what's best for our kids. We want to see them grow up and follow Jesus for a lifetime.

Unfortunately, many Christian teenagers are simply unprepared for the world that is waiting for them. We all know students who have drifted, become disillusioned or just walked away from the faith. Even one heartbreaking story is enough to move us to action. No student should "outgrow" their faith. It doesn't have to be this way.

With the best of intentions, we bubble wrap our kids and create Disney World–like environments for them in our churches, and then wonder why they have no resilience in faith or life. Students are entertained but not prepared. They've had a lot of fun but are not ready to lead.

When the pressure is turned up and the tyranny of tolerance presses in, Christian teenagers tend to wilt if they do not have the confidence that only comes from knowing why they believe what they believe.

Our culture is changing fast and teenagers are confused. The research in this report bears that out. The focus groups Barna conducted with both believing and unbelieving students drove this point home.

When only 34 percent of Gen Z can agree that "lying is morally wrong"— that's a big problem. Not only is our culture deeply confused about moral and spiritual truth, gender and sexuality, but we are getting to the point where no one will listen to someone else's point of view unless they completely agree with them.

Social media keeps us superficially engaged and overwhelmed by data, opinions and information, and Gen Z is now the test case for the long-term effects on identity. Social media is completely reinventing what it means to come of age as a teenager. There's a lot for Gen Z to navigate.

At Impact 360 Institute we have the privilege of teaching, mentoring and equipping teenagers in biblical worldview and leadership. We get to work with students every day in our Christian Gap Year and summer experiences, helping them build a stronger faith.

We hear their questions, doubts and stories, but we wanted a broader lens on this next generation to better understand how Gen Z as a whole sees the world around them.

Working with David Kinnaman and the incredible team at Barna, we commissioned a comprehensive study on Gen Z that would seek to answer significant questions like:

▸ What do they believe about the biggest questions of life?
▸ What unique opportunities and challenges will Christian leaders and parents face while trying to pass on their faith to the next generation?
▸ What do they view as central to their identity?
▸ Will they carry on the Millennial trends Barna has been studying for more than a decade? How are they different?
▸ What is their relationship to faith, parents and institutions?
▸ How have culture and society shaped them?
▸ How are they thinking about what it means to become an adult?

While it can be tempting in our culture to only pay attention to negative trends, there are positive trends as well. What we chose to focus on makes all the difference. Because Jesus is risen and Christianity is true, we have a living hope regardless of the cultural circumstances we find ourselves in. Whether we are in the majority or being marginalized, our charge as followers of Jesus is to be faithful to pass on our faith to the next generation.

As the father of three children I want to keep them *from* dead ends because I want something better *for* them—the kind of joy, confidence and love that only comes from knowing Jesus for a lifetime. The goal is not just to avoid the bad stuff. It's to pursue the good life as God defines it.

Our hope is that the information in these pages makes you aware of the challenges so that you can prepare, but also gives you a way to frame and invest in the opportunities for incredible influence that awaits Gen Z.

PSALM 78:4-7 NLT

We will not hide these truths from our children;
   we will tell the next generation

about the glorious deeds of the Lord,
   about his power and his mighty wonders.

For he issued his laws to Jacob;
   he gave his instructions to Israel.

He commanded our ancestors
   to teach them to their children,

so the next generation might know them—
   even the children not yet born—
   and they in turn will teach their own children.

So each generation should set its hope anew on God,
   not forgetting his glorious miracles
   and obeying his commands.

I N T R O D U C T I O N

By David Kinnaman, President of Barna Group

We live in a complex, accelerated culture.

For a few years now, the Barna team and I have been calling our surrounding culture "digital Babylon," to highlight both the outsized impact of always-connected technology and notable similarities between Judean exiles in Babylon in the sixth century BCE and people of faith today. Not too long ago, North America felt to many (especially white) Christians like Jerusalem to the ancient Judeans: culturally homogeneous, religiously comfortable. But as cultural change has accelerated over the past three decades, many have begun to feel like exiles from their home country. Like the Hebrew exiles, many feel they are living in a place very different from the land of their "tribe."

Jerusalem	Babylon
Faith at the center	Faith at the margins
Monoreligious	Pluralistic
Slower-paced	Accelerated, frenetic
Homogeneity	Diversity
Central control	Open-source
Simpler life	Bitter / sweet tension
Idol: false piety	Idol: fitting in / not missing out

When Daniel, Ezekiel and other Hebrew elites were taken forcibly to Babylon, their view of the world was utterly changed. In order to remain faithful to their calling as the people of God, they had to adjust to a new reality. They had to reimagine what it meant to practice Judaism in a world where the Temple—the epicenter of their religious practice—no longer existed. They had to rethink their own story, to reexamine their understanding of their place in the world and in God's intentions for creation. In response to a worldview-shifting calamity, prophets arose to equip God's people to live in a new world.

Is it possible that many churches are preparing young Christians to face a world that no longer exists? Are we making disciples for Jerusalem when we need to be making disciples for Babylon?

Barna and our research partner, Impact 360 Institute, wanted to begin to understand the next American generation on the cusp of adulthood: Gen Z. Generational analysis is an area of Barna expertise (some might call it an obsession), and our team has suspected for some time that the generation after Millennials would bring different values and assumptions to the cultural table—and this expansive research project was our first chance to test that hypothesis.

Our theory was correct: Gen Z teens are not just mini-Millennials.

Born between 1999 and 2015, Gen Z—as we're calling them for now—is between 69 and 70 million children and teens, the largest American generation yet. For our first in-depth research with this population, researchers focused on youth ages 13 to 18, U.S. adults 19 and older (for comparison), and committed Christian parents and youth pastors for insights on how they are discipling Gen Z. (For a complete research methodology, see Appendix B.)

Our goal for the research and for the report you're holding is a first look at Generation Z, including their:

▸ **Identity:** how they define themselves, what makes them who they are
▸ **Worldview:** their spiritual and moral beliefs, their understanding of what life is about
▸ **Motivations:** their life goals and priorities, what they think is important
▸ **Views on faith and church:** what they think about Christianity and Christian communities

In these pages, we share our findings and offer insights from our researchers, as well as from outside contributors whose expertise shine different angles of light on the "spiritual blank slate" that is Gen Z. We believe Christ's followers have something essential to offer this diverse, fluid, empathetic, anxious generation growing up in digital Babylon: hope.

Let's get to know them together.

Making Gen Z | The Forces Forming a Generation

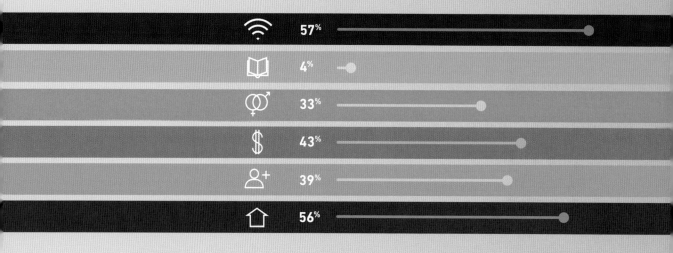

57%

4%

33%

43%

39%

56%

TECHNOLOGY

The internet is at the core of Gen Z's development, a uniquely powerful influence on their worldview, mental health, daily schedule, sleep patterns, relationships and more. Devices are almost constantly on their person and on their minds.

WORLDVIEW

The worldview of Gen Z (and, in turn, their moral code) is highly inclusive and individualistic. This diverse, open-minded group of young people is sensitive to others' feelings and experiences, and wary of asserting any one view as right or wrong.

IDENTITY

Their assorted views on gender identity and expression are just one way teens are wrestling with how to accept and affirm other people, to create "safe space" where each person can be herself or himself without feeling threatened or judged.

SECURITY

Gen Z has come of age in a post-9/11 nation reeling from the 2008 recession, and many teens are anxious about their future. Their goals revolve around professional success and financial security, and a majority says their ultimate aim is "to be happy"—which a plurality defines as financial success.

DIVERSITY

As the most racially, religiously and sexually diverse generation in American history, Gen Z expects people to have different beliefs and experiences, and they seem to have a greater appreciation for social inclusiveness compared to generations before them.

Teens ages 13–18, n=1,490, Nov. 4–16, 2016. Teens, ages 13–18, n =507, July 7-18, 2017.

More than half **USE SCREEN MEDIA FOUR HOURS** or more on an average day.[1]

Out of 69 million children and teens in Gen Z, **JUST 4 PERCENT HAVE A BIBLICAL WORLDVIEW.** *

One-third of teens says **GENDER IS HOW A PERSON FEELS INSIDE**, not their birth sex.

Many believe **HAPPINESS IS DEFINED BY FINANCIAL SUCCESS.**

Two in five teens **INTERACT WITH PEOPLE WHO ARE DIFFERENT FROM THEM** compared to just one-quarter of Boomers.

Half say **PARENTS ARE THEIR PRIMARY ROLE MODEL,** but only one-third that family is core to their identity.

PARENTS

As the offspring of mostly Gen X parents, many in Gen Z appear to have a complicated dynamic with their family. They admire their parents, but most don't feel family relationships are central to their sense of self—a major departure from other generations.

*For a complete list of beliefs included in the biblical worldview profile, see Appendix B.

 AT A GLANCE

Teens 13 to 18 years old are twice as likely
as adults to say they are atheist (13% vs. 6%).
Only three in five identify as Christian, compared to two-thirds of adults (59% vs. 68%).

About half of Gen Z is nonwhite.
They are the most racially and ethnically diverse generation in American history.

Half say happiness is their ultimate goal in life (51%).
What does happiness entail? For 43 percent of Gen Z, financial success.

More than half of teens use screen media
four or more hours per day (57%).[1]
One-quarter reports looking at a screen eight or more hours on an average day (26%).

One-third reports being bullied online (33%),
compared to only one in five adults (20%).

1

The World
According to Gen Z

During their childhood and early adult years, each generation collectively experiences a handful of events or cultural trends that serve to shape their generational ethos. For Boomers it was—among other things—post-WWII prosperity and the rise of the consumer economy, the sexual revolution, the Vietnam War and the Civil Rights movement. Gen X was formed in part by the *Challenger* disaster, the end of the Cold War, no-fault divorce and the personal computer. The 9/11 attacks and the subsequent War on Terror loom large for Millennials, but perhaps not as large as the Internet, video gaming and mobile technology, globalization and diversity, and the consumer mindset of their Boomer parents.

The oldest members of Gen Z are now on the cusp of adulthood. Here are six trends that are working together to form their shared worldview, based on recent scholarly research and new Barna data.

1. They Are Screenagers

One of the defining influences on Gen Z is that they have come of age in a world saturated by digital technology and mediated by mobile devices. Many admit to having experienced "nomophobia," a feeling of anxiety any time they are separated from their mobile phone. They can't remember a time before the Internet; they're "digital natives," a term popularized by Marc Prensky, a writer and speaker in the field of education.[2] Prensky, among many others, believes the ubiquitous presence of digital technology has changed the way young people process and interact with information. The changes are so pervasive that another nickname for Gen Z is "screenagers."

Social scientist Jean Twenge has dubbed them "iGen," making explicit the nearly symbiotic relationship between teens and their internet-connected mobile devices.[3] Beyond the effects of a curtailed attention span, Twenge believes smartphones have "radically changed every aspect of teenager's lives." She argues that, though they are physically safer, they are psychologically

> Gen Z has come of age in a world saturated by digital technology and mediated by mobile devices

more vulnerable. For instance, teens are less likely to leave their homes, drink alcohol, get their driver's license and go out on dates than generations before them at the same age. But while teen pregnancies, for example, are rarer than ever, rates of teen suicide and depression have skyrocketed. Twenge believes this is because teens live their social life on their phones, and much of that time is spent "in their room, alone and often distressed." Teens are hanging out with their friends less; basketball courts and town pools have "all been replaced by virtual spaces accessed through apps and the web."

Smartphone use is cutting into teens' sleeping patterns, with many getting less than seven hours a night. Many teens and young adults sleep with their phone and check social media just before they go to sleep, then reach for it the minute they wake in the morning. More than half of 13- to 18-year-olds in a recent national study admit they use a screen four or more hours a day; one-quarter admits to *eight* or more hours, making smartphone, tablet or other screen use their top daily activity.

Gen Z Hours On Screen Media

(each day)

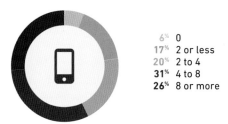

6%	0
17%	2 or less
20%	2 to 4
31%	4 to 8
26%	8 or more

"The Common Sense Census: Media Use by Tweens and Teens," 2015. This includes watching TV, movies and online video; playing video, computer and mobile games; using social media; using the internet; reading and listening to music.

But it's not only a lack of sleep and its associated problems that could spell trouble; mobile technology itself is potentially making an irreversible impact on young brains. The truth is, it's too soon to tell. According to *The New York Times*, "Though smartphones seem ubiquitous in daily life, they are actually so new that researchers are just beginning to understand what the devices may do to the brain."[4] According to a paper published in the *Journal of Individual Psychology*:

Generation Z's lower cognitive regions, which stimulate impulse, are constantly being activated by the bombardment of neurological arousal provided by text messages, Facebook updates, and video games. At the same time, the so-called Google culture of learning—finding answers to any question within seconds—continues to change the way Generation Z youth concentrate, write, and reflect. . . . Their capacity for linear thinking has been replaced by a new mode of thinking, in which they need to take in and dish out information in a fast, disjointed, overlapping manner. [5]

Other researchers have begun to take stock of the neurological implications for memory, problem solving, concentration, addiction and risk-taking behaviors among teens and adults.[6]

So what are screenagers doing on their phones and other web-connected screens all day? Gaming, consuming entertainment such as streaming video, and engaging on social media like Snapchat, Tumblr, Twitter, Instagram, Facebook and others. According to a national survey of teens, 45 percent report using social media every day, and among all 13- to 18-year-olds the average amount of time per day is more than one hour (some are engaging far longer and some not at all).[7]

For the most part, teens use social media for the same activities as adults: connecting with friends and family members, sharing photos or videos or catching up on the latest news. However, Gen Z is much more likely than older generations to use social media to branch outside of their existing personal network. More than half say they also use these media to meet new people or connect with celebrities or consumer brands. They are twice as likely as adults to say "I enjoy interacting online with people I have not met in real life" (18% vs. 9% all adults).

Among teens who use social media, seven out of 10 say they are happy with the amount of time they spend engaging with these technologies (69%). That's a slightly larger percentage than among Millennials, the generation just ahead of them; 64 percent of young adults 19 to 33 say they are satisfied with their social media use. Similarly, teens are less likely than adults to agree that "social media sometimes interferes with my face-to-face interactions." Even if it *is* interfering, only 12 percent say they notice it much, compared to about one in five adults (20%). Perhaps this is a result of having never known a world where social media doesn't exist. For this generation, it is as comfortable as a second skin.

How I Use Social Media: Gen Z vs. Adults

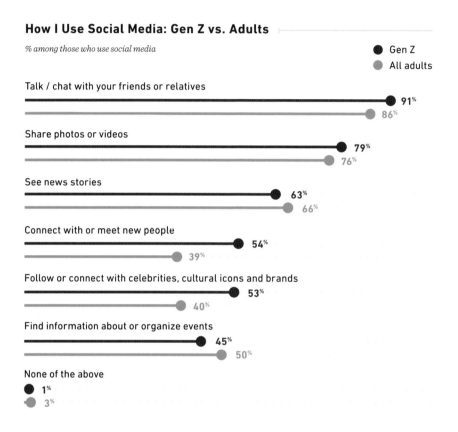

% among those who use social media

● Gen Z
● All adults

Talk / chat with your friends or relatives
● 91%
● 86%

Share photos or videos
● 79%
● 76%

See news stories
● 63%
● 66%

Connect with or meet new people
● 54%
● 39%

Follow or connect with celebrities, cultural icons and brands
● 53%
● 40%

Find information about or organize events
● 45%
● 50%

None of the above
● 1%
● 3%

Trusted Information Sources

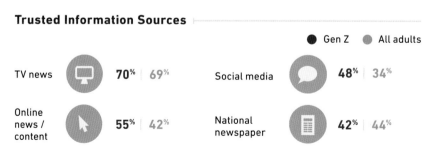

● Gen Z ● All adults

	Gen Z	All adults
TV news	70%	69%
Online news / content	55%	42%
Social media	48%	34%
National newspaper	42%	44%

U.S. teens ages 13–18, *n*=1,490, Nov. 4–16, 2016. U.S. adults 19 and older, *n*=1,517, Nov. 4–16, 2016.

Gen Z, along with Millennials, are more likely than older generations to think social media is a good place to discuss opinions and ideas, and to trust information they encounter online. Indeed, for many of them the better question might be, "Where else would I go?"

Researcher Danah Boyd is more optimistic than Twenge and others about the effects of mobile devices and social media use among teens. Boyd sees these technologies, which are now part of everyday life for young people, as tools for extending the pleasure of connecting with friends in real time.[8] She believes that in-person time with friends is made difficult by restrictive parenting, so online spaces have become new public spaces. Social media makes friendship the key organizing principle of young people's social worlds and also provides teens with new opportunities to participate in public life. She argues that young people have more power and capacity than adults give them credit for. Social media allows them to create networked communities where they actively take part in self-expression and identity formation. These new "networked publics," as Boyd calls them, are ultimately opportunities, not dangers, for teenagers.

Over time that may turn out to be true. But at least for now, these "opportunities" appear to adversely affect kids' happiness—which is ironic, considering the premium Gen Z puts on being happy. Fully half strongly agree that "happiness is my ultimate goal in life" (51%) compared to 44 percent of all adults. Yet research shows that more time with screen activities is consistently linked to less happiness. Despite the promise of connection, social media exacerbates loneliness and dislocation, and appears to increase rates of depression. As Jean Twenge reports, "In 2011, for the first time in 24 years, the teen suicide rate was higher than the teen homicide rate."[9] The psychological distress of smartphone and social media use is related to the fear of missing out ("FOMO"), especially when those social encounters are documented online so relentlessly. Those who aren't invited are keenly aware, through social media, of what is happening without them, leading to feelings of exclusion and loneliness. Those who post are also affected, anxiously waiting for the affirmation of comments and "likes"; this is most acute among young women.

In her book *The Happiness Effect*, Donna Freitas argues that the pressure to appear happy and successful online not only fosters inauthenticity, but can actually make people less happy.[10] As one student told Freitas, "People share

Half of teens agree that "happiness is my ultimate goal in life"

● Gen Z
● Millennials
● Gen X
● Boomers

❝ Looking at other people's posts often makes me feel bad about the way I look.

31%
30%
20%
4%

❝ Looking at other people's posts often makes me feel bad about the lack of excitement in my own life.

39%
34%
24%
8%

❝ I have experienced bullying on social media.

33%
29%
20%
12%

U.S. teens ages 13–18, *n*=1,490, Nov. 4–16, 2016.
U.S. adults 19 and older, *n*=1,517, Nov. 4–16, 2016.

the best version of themselves, and we compare that to the worst version of ourselves."

Barna data validates that student's claim. Agreement with negative statements about social media (see sidebar) increases in each successive generation, and is strongest among Gen Z. (And women in each generation are more likely than men to report these feelings.)

In order to keep up with their peers, members of Gen Z create a personal brand by "manicuring" their online presence, driven by the knowledge that they are constantly being watched, not only by their peers, but by future employers. This is an exhausting way to live, but they don't feel they can stop. Social media is where they feel most "seen"—but the version of themselves that is being seen isn't authentic. This vicious dynamic is familiar to anyone who has ever been in high school—the pressure to act a certain way to fit in—but now there is no escaping it. There's no time or place where teens are really safe. Even alone in their bedroom at night, many can't stop scrolling through others' photos or videos. They feel pressured by the temptation to post something. There's just no escape.

Inauthenticity and constant self-monitoring are not the only psychological risks, however. In the Barna study, one-third of 13- to 18-year-olds report having been on the receiving end of online bullying (33%)—far more than older generations, though nearly on par with Millennials. From the study published in the *Journal of Individual Psychology*:

The difference between Generation Z cyberbullies and bullies of other generations is that Generation Z no longer sees the immediate physical consequences of—or immediate feedback from—these maladjusted

(Continued on page 24)

Q & A WITH
DONNA FREITAS

SCHOLAR, AUTHOR AND SPEAKER

Donna lectures at universities across the U.S. on her work about college students. Over the years she has written for national newspapers and magazines, including *The Wall Street Journal, The New York Times, The Boston Globe* and *The Washington Post*. She's currently a non-resident research associate at the Center for Religion and Society at Notre Dame. In 2008 Donna published *Sex and the Soul: Juggling Sexuality, Spirituality, Romance and Religion on America's College Campuses*. Her latest book, *The Happiness Effect: How Social Media Is Driving a Generation to Appear Perfect at Any Cost*, is based on research from her new study about social media and how it affects the ways college students construct identity, make meaning in the world and navigate relationships.

Since happiness is the ultimate life goal for so many teens, researchers wanted to know what that means to them. Barna asked Gen Z what happiness "looks like," using images and word labels. Just under half select the image of money paired with the word "success." The theme of success also came up in our Q&A with Dr. Freitas.

SUCCESS 43%

FAMILY 20%

EDUCATION 23%

HEALTH 6%

SPIRITUAL 8%

Yes, the goal for their social media presence seems to be about appearing happy at every turn—with all profiles that are attached to their real names. Appearing successful, appearing positive, never showing that you're vulnerable, never showing that you've failed at anything, never showing that you're sad. There's a kind of constant performance that's expected on social media. The students I interviewed spoke of learning that the appearance of happiness is more important than actually being happy.

Part of the problem is that parents, teachers and career counselors, as early as middle school, are telling young adults and their kids that what they post on social media will follow them the rest of their lives; that it might come back to haunt them. These warnings are everywhere, and with good reason: College admissions officers and potential employers *are* checking young people's social media presence, so being aware of that fact is not crazy. And what they post *will* follow them. But many of the students I speak with take awareness to the level of fear. "If I post one wrong thing, I may get turned down by my dream college. Just one picture could cost me a job in the future."

The result is a growing gap between who they are and what they post. Social media is less about interacting with people around them, and more about pleasing those in power, because those in power will go searching their names and finding those profiles. This generation is acutely aware of that fact. And I think they're disappointed that a lot of social media isn't about having fun, playing around and socializing, but about presenting themselves to people who have power over their future.

The success we're teaching young people to post about on social media is achievement. Then, once it's posted, it's no longer about the achievement itself but about the "likes" that post gets. It's a numbers game. If the algorithms work in your favor, you get the most likes, the most attention. Otherwise you're invisible, right? You aren't seen.

Students have shared with me specific, numbers-related goals for their social media presence—100 likes or 1,000 likes, or a certain number of "friends." There is a pervasive sense that social media is a competition, and many students feel bad when they don't win. Many seem to really believe they will finally feel fulfilled if they meet their numbers goals.

The sad thing is, they *like* social media when it helps them stay connected with people. But at the same time, they feel they're competing with those same people.

That's the million-dollar question, isn't it? As a culture one thing we didn't do well before social media started dominating every aspect of our lives is think about the ethics of how we use it. For instance, is it okay for college admissions officers or future bosses to use our social media pages as a proxy reference?

On one level, it makes sense why admissions people or interviewers do it. People don't think about the ethics, they just want more information about a job candidate or a potential on-campus RA. And now investigating social media has become the norm.

But could it be that we need to respect young people's privacy? It's as if we're all parents who have found our kid's diary lying open on the table and didn't even stop to think whether we should read it—we just picked it up and started reading because it was there. As a culture, I think we need to ask if that is really okay.

On top of that, most people haven't figured out how to have a healthy relationship with social media. Many people haven't even asked the question about what a healthy relationship would look like, and before they know it, they find themselves feeling terrible about themselves or feeling compulsive and addicted. Or all of the above. It's only then that they begin to ask—and many students I've spoken with have concluded they just don't know.

I think we could start by going back to the social aspect of social media. Are these media really designed to help people connect, or are they designed to ramp up competition? I think we know the answer, and maybe the horse is already out of the gate and there's no going back. But the questions are worth asking.

We've just gotten ahead of ourselves, and in our rush we've gotten ourselves into a really complicated situation. There's this big rush to make sure there's Wi-Fi everywhere, even in our outdoor spaces. Everywhere we go—every coffee shop, every restaurant, every campus, every school, every inch of our community. And there's a rush to use social media for everyday communication, with very little reflection on the possible consequences.

Is there anything the faith community can do to help?

There are so many churches in the United States that are social-media obsessed. It's a huge communication tool for many churches, especially younger churches, and for many faith groups on campus.

Many students feel trapped in every dimension of their lives to continue using social media, even though they don't know how to have a healthy relationship with it. They can't escape. Their teachers or bosses require them to use social media—and now many churches do, too. If you're not on social media, you don't know what's happening. You're not a part of the community. And I think faith communities should think long and hard about the ways we've made social media so pervasive, when what many students need is at least an hour a week when they are forced to unplug. They want space and time away from their devices, even if they say otherwise, because many have a hard time making that decision themselves. Do we have to make it harder for them?

behaviors, because the Internet provides the "safety" of anonymity. The instant and impulsive nature of Internet cyberbullying is a phenomenon entirely unique to Generation Z youth, and it allows for socially disinterested behaviors to proliferate in ways we have never before seen.[11]

Whether, as this generation grows into adulthood, ubiquitous technology will prove to be a greater blessing than a curse remains to be seen. Either way, it will have made an indelible mark.

2. Their Worldview Is Post-Christian

It is not breaking news that the influence of Christianity in the United States is waning. Historical Barna data show that rates of church attendance, religious affiliation, belief in God, prayer and Bible-reading have been dropping

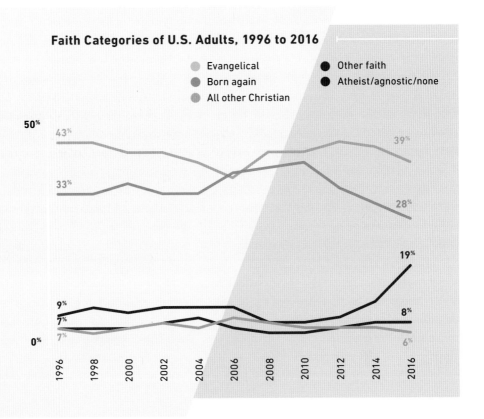

Faith Categories of U.S. Adults, 1996 to 2016

- Evangelical
- Born again
- All other Christian
- Other faith
- Atheist/agnostic/none

for decades. Consequently, the role of religion in public life has also diminished, and the Church no longer holds the cultural authority it wielded in times past. These are unique days for the Church in America as it learns what it means to flourish in a post-Christian era.

There are a few different ways we can look at the post-Christian phenomenon. Using a classification of faith based on widely accepted, orthodox Christian beliefs, Barna developed a profile of people with a "biblical world-view."* The percentage of people whose beliefs qualify them for a biblical worldview declines in each successively younger generation: 10 percent of Boomers, 7 percent of Gen X and 6 percent of Millennials have a biblical worldview, compared to only 4 percent of Gen Z.

Americans' beliefs are becoming more post-Christian and, concurrently, religious identity is changing. (See previous page.) Within the self-identified Christian population, the percentage that qualifies as evangelical according to Barna's definition, which is based on nine points of theological and personal belief, has remained stable over the past two decades. However, those whom Barna classifies as "born again" (who say they have faith in Jesus and believe salvation comes through faith alone) have dwindled, especially in the last six years. During the same period, the percentage of those with no religious affiliation has risen, mostly thanks to the growing number of Americans under 50 who say they are "none of the above."

In Gen Z we see more of the same trends, except for one glaring difference: The percentage of Gen Z that identifies as atheist is *double* that of U.S. adults. We'll dig into this massive shift in an upcoming chapter. For now, here is a generational breakdown of how Americans identify today:

The percentage of people with a biblical worldview declines in each generation:

Boomers 10%
Gen X 7%
Millennials 6%
Gen Z 4%

U.S. Religious Identity 2018

Which of the following best describes your religious faith?

- Christian (non-Catholic)
- Catholic
- Other faith
- Agnostic
- Atheist
- None of these

	Gen Z	Millennials	Gen X	Boomers	Elders
Christian (non-Catholic)	42%	44%	43%	48%	51%
Catholic	17%	21%	22%	27%	24%
Other faith	7%	5%	5%	5%	4%
Agnostic	8%	8%	7%	4%	5%
Atheist	13%	7%	6%	5%	6%
None of these	14%	15%	17%	11%	9%

U.S. teens ages 13–18, n=1,490, Nov. 4–16, 2016. U.S. adults 19 and older, n=1,517, Nov. 4–16, 2016.
*For a complete list of beliefs included in the biblical worldview profile, see Appendix B.

Many in Generation Z, more than in generations before them, are a spiritual blank slate. They are drawn to things spiritual, but their starting point is vastly different from previous generations, many of whom received a basic education on the Bible and Christianity. The worldview of Gen Z, by contrast, is truly post-Christian. They were not born into a Christian culture, and it shows.

You will notice throughout this study that we refer to various faith categories. These groups are a combination of religious self-identification and Christian beliefs and practices. When researchers segment Gen Z by faith, we find that, while a majority of teens still self-identifies as "Christian" (58%), only 43 percent have recently attended church, and just one in 11 is an "engaged Christian," with beliefs and practices that put faith front-and-center in their lives.* This is a significantly smaller percentage than their grandparents: 14 percent of Boomers are engaged Christians.

> Many in Gen Z, more than in generations before them, are a spiritual blank slate

Gen Z Faith Segments

9% Engaged Christian
33% Churched Christian
16% Unchurched Christian
7% Other faith
34% No religious affiliation

U.S. teens ages 13–18, n=1,490, Nov. 4–16, 2016.

In *Meet Generation Z,* James Emery White agrees that Gen Z is the first "truly post-Christian generation."[12] The rise of the religiously unaffiliated, or "nones," is symptomatic of a growing cultural apathy toward religion. He suggests that nominal Christians—those who identify culturally with the name if not with the commitment—are no longer the "center" between the poles of the religious and the atheist; the culture is secularizing, and those in the middle are shifting away from the religious pole. "As the cultural cost of being a Christian increases, people who were once Christian only in name likely have started to identify as nones, disintegrating the 'ideological bridge' between unbelievers and believers."[13]

As we will see in later chapters, the bridge between believing and unbelieving teens is nearly nonexistent.

*For a complete definition of "engaged Christian" and other Barna categories, see Appendix B.

3. "Safe Spaces" Are Normal

As we will see, Gen Z teens do not like to make people feel bad—which is not, in and of itself, a problem. Their collective aversion to causing offense is the natural product of a pluralistic, inclusive culture that frowns on passing judgment that might provoke negative feelings in the judged. Two timely examples of this value are trigger warnings (written notices that content could provoke negative emotions such as fear or anger) and safe spaces (designated areas where such content is banned, either online or in physical space). The original intent of these concepts was to encourage awareness of content that could be psychologically harmful to victims of trauma or those with mental illness. Over time, however, use of trigger warnings has expanded in media and in classrooms. It's not unusual to see notices about material that might be offensive or simply emotionally distressing. Safe spaces, in turn, have become designated areas not only to avoid information that could induce or remind one of trauma, but also to opt out of discussions that may in any way upset or provoke an individual.

The creation of trigger warnings and safe spaces was inspired by empathy, compassion and sound psychological principles—yet, when misused or overused, they ultimately do more harm than good. As Alan Levinovitz writes:

> There is a very real danger that these efforts [to institute trigger warnings and safe spaces] will become overzealous and render opposing opinions taboo. Instead of dialogues in which everyone is fairly represented, campus conversations about race, gender, and religion will devolve into monologues about the virtues of tolerance and diversity. Even though academic debate takes place in a community, it is also combat. Combat can hurt. It is literally offensive. Without offense there is no antagonistic dialogue, no competitive marketplace, and no chance to change your mind.[14]

In their book *Good Faith,* Barna president David Kinnaman and Gabe Lyons argue, "Protecting people from ideas they'd rather not hear is not only laughable but also ultimately harmful to society. Religious liberty and freedom of speech are rights that can only be put to the test at the distressing intersection of differing ideas. If we run away from that crossroads, these

> Gen Z's collective aversion to causing offense is the natural product of a pluralistic, inclusive culture that frowns on passing judgment

freedoms are simply hypothetical."[15] (Kinnaman and Lyons were writing about Millennials, but the phenomenon has only grown more extreme since *Good Faith* was published.)

In focus groups for this study, Barna researchers heard time and again from teens, "I don't know; I'm so confused" and similar remarks in answer to seemingly basic questions like "Who was Jesus?" (You will also see in this report that "not sure" is a popular option on a majority of multiple-choice questions.) Many teens are deeply reluctant to make declarative statements about anything that could cause offense, and thus they struggle with anxiety and indecision when it's time to give an answer, or time to act on it. In many ways they are the postmodern version of ancient Nineveh, about which God asked the prophet Jonah, "Should I not pity that great city, in which there are more than 120,000 persons who do not know their right hand from their left?" (Jonah 4:11, ESV).

4. Real Safety Is a Myth

Although the tolerant inoffensiveness of "safe spaces" is a norm for Gen Z, the underlying anxiety that so many experience has led to a collective suspicion that true security is unattainable, or at least outside their control.

The *Harry Potter* books are, for many Millennials, a touchstone. Young adults came of age with Harry, who fought against and ultimately defeated the evil Lord Voldemort with the help of his friends and his magical abilities. If magic is a metaphor for inborn talent and "specialness," Harry's journey could be seen as an aspirational prototype for many twentysomethings—who, generationally speaking, are interested in working together to defeat the evils of social injustice.

Gen Z's social awareness began to dawn right around the Great Recession of 2008

Gen Z are not so optimistic, and are not altogether clear on what evils need defeating. Their social awareness began to dawn right around the Great Recession of 2008, and there is a dystopian slant on the books and movies popular among today's YA audience that is very much at odds with the epic hero fantasy of Harry Potter. Many of these books are set in a post-apocalyptic future in which humanity has nearly destroyed itself and the earth. The resulting violence and loss of freedom offer bleak, authoritarian visions of humanity's future. The best that the heroines of *The Hunger Games* and the *Divergent* trilogy can hope for is a quiet country life tinged by trauma and a violent death, respectively. Teens have never personally experienced a time when the norm was a dependable job with a livable wage and a reliable social safety net. After seeing their (mainly Gen X) parents struggle in the workforce only to earn financial stress, many young people express a strong sense of responsibility and entrepreneurial drive, likely in an effort to feel more in control of their future.

Financial expectations are only one of the cultural norms that have drastically shifted over the last several decades. Most in Gen Z do not remember the years before 9/11. They do not recall ever having lived in a country at peace. "As a group raised in constant war, contemporary youth may view the world with the belief that the world is 'unsafe,' yet at the same time, they may have greater global awareness as a result."[16] Between the financial crisis and perpetual war, they are apt to be distrustful of the future. According to analysis in *Forbes*:

> Generation Z never had the luxury of a threat-free perspective so they've been forced to view life through a more guarded lens from the start. . . . The wary worldview of this group is further shaped by generation X parents, who came of age in the post-Watergate and Vietnam years amidst a time of economic and global uncertainty.[17]

Complementing, or perhaps exacerbating, their controlling streak are shifting cultural expectations about sexuality and gender identity. Not only are they collectively supportive of those who identify as LGBTQ but, as we'll see in a later chapter, they are also more likely than adults to personally express some level of sexual fluidity or non-binary identity.[18] As far as Gen Z is concerned, when it comes to gender expression and sexual orientation, there is no norm—and that can be deeply unsettling. If even your own body cannot reliably represent you to the world, is *anything* trustworthy?

5. They Are Diverse

As *The Hunger Games* and *Divergent*—not to mention *Wonder Woman, Moana* and *Hidden Figures*—demonstrate, the Age of Women in entertainment may have arrived at long last. And female success is ascendant elsewhere, too.

Most in Gen Z do not remember the years before 9/11. They do not recall ever having lived in a country at peace

Where men at one time went to college in proportions far higher than women—58 percent to 42 percent as recently as the 1970s—the ratio has now almost exactly reversed. This fall, women will comprise more than 56 percent of students on campuses nationwide, according to the U.S. Department of Education. Some 2.2 million fewer men than women will be enrolled in college this year. And the trend shows no sign of abating.[19]

Demographics in This Study, by Generation

Respondents could choose all that apply.

● White   ● Asian
● Black   ● Other
● Hispanic

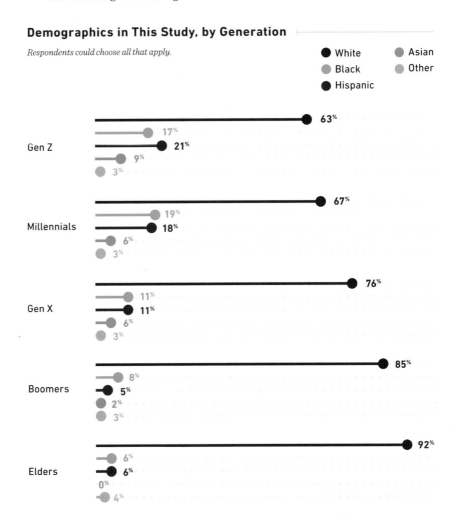

Gen Z
- 63%
- 17%
- 21%
- 9%
- 3%

Millennials
- 67%
- 19%
- 18%
- 6%
- 3%

Gen X
- 76%
- 11%
- 11%
- 6%
- 3%

Boomers
- 85%
- 8%
- 5%
- 2%
- 3%

Elders
- 92%
- 6%
- 6%
- 0%
- 4%

U.S. teens ages 13–18, *n*=1,490, Nov. 4–16, 2016. U.S. adults 19 and older, *n*=1,517, Nov. 4–16, 2016.

(Continued on page 34)

Q & A WITH IRENE CHO

PROGRAM MANAGER AT FULLER YOUTH INSTITUTE

Irene serves as the program manager for the Fuller Youth Institute (FYI). She holds a Master of Divinity from Talbot Theological Seminary and a BA in Christian education from Biola University, and is a PhD student in Fuller's School of Intercultural Studies. At FYI, Irene is the point person for Urban Youth Ministry training and resources. Having served over 25 years in youth ministry, her passion is for the misfits of the world and to bring the gospel message to those who seem to fall through the cracks. In her minimal spare time, Irene enjoys a great book, movie or television show, hanging out with friends, former students and her new husband and, of course, getting some sleep.

The research turned up lots of evidence that urban teens, compared to suburban and rural young people, often experience a wider spectrum of diversity on a daily basis—cultural, sexual, moral, religious and so on. They tend to know more people who are different from them in some significant way. What unique challenges and opportunities do you think this poses for discipleship?

One unique challenge urban teens face is how intersectional every part of their life is. For them, diversity is not just about race; it's a complex intersection of values, language, culture, family structures, interpersonal dynamics, customs, finances and education.

Our urban students' lives are the focal point where all these different highways converge in a massive interchange with no traffic lights or rules. As you can imagine, it gets messy fast. Conflict is inevitable, which makes conversations, relationships and discipleship difficult.

However, this *intersectionality* also creates one of the greatest opportunities for discipleship. This freeway interchange forces diverse cultures and values to come together in once place. The key is to slow down and take a good long look at the different ideas and people swirling around you. By slowing down, engaging in intentional dialogue and doing the hard work of listening to understand the people around you, the intersections can be transformed from perilous to disciple-making.

Empathy is really the key. And you can't practice empathy if you're trapped in your own car going 90 mph with only your own destination in mind. The key is to slow down, get out, ask questions, be a passenger and deeply understand what each person in your ministry values, contributes and needs.

A second unique challenge is the phenomenon of code-switching. Code-switching is shifting your language or behavior in order to fit a certain social situation—and urban students become masters at it to survive. For example, a second-gen Korean teenager will speak to their parents in English, but with a Korean accent. They will use mannerisms and gestures common to their ethnic culture. Then they'll turn around and speak in English with zero accent to their American friends, and hold their body completely differently. This is code-switching. Research indicates that code-switching can have negative effects on young people, in particular with identity development. Many urban teens experience a sense of either not belonging or having dual identities. They're one type of person with one set of friends, and a different person with another set of friends.

On the flip side, this challenge also presents a unique opportunity for discipleship. Jesus himself was constantly code-switching when interacting with diverse people from the devout religious leaders to the disciples, from the bleeding woman to Gentiles. Jesus himself had many intersections in his life, and showed us what discipleship with the other looks like in a complicated and challenging environment.

One thing Jesus modeled in this complex context was the concept of the "close inner circle." He spoke to the masses, but had a small circle of disciples that he confided in and shared with. The church has a discipleship opportunity to be this space for urban teens who need an inner circle to process their multiple worlds, a "home base" where they can breathe a sigh of relief in the midst of daily code-switching, that helps them find identity and belonging in a perpetually unstable environment.

When it comes to their priorities for the future, a majority of churchgoing teens, along with their generational cohort, is most interested in educational achievement and financial independence. Only one in five expresses a desire to "become more mature spiritually" by age 30. One in four says they want to get married by then; just one in six says they want to have children. This is pretty much the case for all teens, regardless of faith background or practice. What, if anything, can parents, churches and youth leaders do to help Christian teens reprioritize?

We have been exploring this specific question at the Fuller Youth Institute through both our Sticky Faith and Growing Young research. What gives us hope is that a lot of young people *do* prioritize their faith, the church and, most importantly, the gospel of Jesus. Yet, there is sometimes a disconnect between the faith and gospel teens are prioritizing, and the faith and gospel their church is prioritizing.

Our research shows that churches sometimes, whether intentionally or not, present a predominantly legalistic gospel that young people translate into a checklist of do's and don'ts. This is what Dallas Willard called the "gospel of sin management." This checklist leads many young people to experience a burdened life of guilt, shame and failure, instead of a thriving relationship with Jesus that transforms their life and bears fruit.

It's because of this many young people depart from the church in search of communities that have a more holistic understanding of the gospel. How do we change that? FYI's research reveals that providing young people with safe spaces to ask difficult questions, express doubts, learn how to integrate with their world and engage with internal struggle is absolutely crucial to cultivating faith. Doubt is not what kills faith; silence is. When we don't allow young people to explore challenging ideas and questions, we inadvertently preach a small Jesus rather than the Lord and Savior of the world. Instead of silencing young people, it's imperative that leaders and parents help young people develop critical thoughts about faith and life. Sadly, many young people in our research shared that church was the last place they felt safe as they wrestled with their identity, future and life.

We need to shift our teaching methods from rote memorization and regurgitation to experiential dialogue and growth. How can we do this? One of the greatest gifts my mother gave me was the skill of asking good questions. She asked me insightful, introspective questions, which in turn taught me how to ask better questions of myself, my faith and relationship with Jesus, and how that all intertwines with the world. And most importantly, she did not always provide the answers. Rather, she utilized the method Jesus uses throughout the Gospels. It's amazing that Jesus never answers closed-ended questions with closed-ended answers. Instead, he always elevates conversations with open-ended questions.* He helps people find their own answers by asking questions, allowing people to process their faith journey and arrive at answers, rather than forcing answers. This is an extremely important method we need to utilize in our everyday conversations with young people. Our culture is too focused on providing answers.

Asking deep, introspective questions can initially feel unsafe for leaders and parents, and the journey may take longer; it's fraught with uncertainty and tension. But while it *takes* longer, it will *last* longer. It will be deeper. And it's what young people want. Providing closed-ended answers is more like a quick diet: speedy initial results with little long-term change. Instead, we ought to go the difficult route of a lifestyle change: having faith and trust that the Holy Spirit is working through the questions young people are asking, engaging with them and allowing them the space to wrestle and realize.

Questions and processing is what will help young people integrate their faith with life, and ultimately make faith a priority now and in the future.

*From *Love Is an Orientation*, Andrew Marin.

Complete acceptance,
and even elevation,
of non-male and
nonwhite is a
generational marker

Complete acceptance, and even elevation, of non-male and nonwhite is a generational marker. Gen Z "are experiencing radical changes in . . . family, sexuality, and gender. They live in multigenerational households, and the fastest-growing demographic within their age group is multi-racial."[20]

The Census Bureau found that 48% of Gen Z is non-Caucasian. The next most-diverse generation is the Millennials, 44% of whom are non-Caucasian. Members of Gen Z are also the most likely to say they have friends of a different sexual orientation (59%, versus 53% of Millennials and smaller percentages of the older generations).[21]

Racial demographics from Barna's research closely mirror federal data trends (see chart on page 30). The kindergarteners who started school in 2016 were the first American class in which minority ethnicities made up a majority of students, and whites the minority. For the next generation on the brink of American adulthood, different is ordinary.

6. Their Parents Are Double-Minded

In assessing the parenting approach of Gen Z's mostly Gen X parents, observers seem to fall into one of two camps. In one are those who believe Gen Z's caregivers are of the "helicopter" variety: overprotective, hypermanaging and fearful. On the other are those who suggest just the opposite: that most Gen X parents are, in fact, *under*protective because they are so keen to avoid the helicopter label. The truth, however, may be a combination of both extremes, a parenting dichotomy: overprotective in some ways and underprotective in others (especially in digital spaces). The apostle James warns against being "double-minded" because wavering and vacillation make a person (or parent) unstable. Could that be what's going on here?

Those weighing in on the first side of the debate include investigative journalist Hannah Rosin. She argues that "a preoccupation with safety has stripped childhood of independence, risk taking, and discovery—without making it safer."[22] She believes childhood norms have shifted dramatically in a single generation, with parents becoming significantly more protective over a short period of time. For instance, "in 1971, 80 percent of third-graders walked to school alone. By 1990, that measure had dropped to 9 percent, and now it's even lower." The problem is, the world is not more dangerous; we just perceive it to be that way. She goes on to suggest that parental supervision is now overwrought. The result is a "continuous and ultimately dramatic decline in children's opportunities to play and explore in their own chosen ways." As a result, children have become "less emotionally expressive, less energetic, less talkative and verbally expressive, less humorous, less imaginative, less unconventional, less lively and passionate, less perceptive, less apt to connect seemingly irrelevant things, less synthesizing, and less likely to see things from a different angle." Ultimately, suggests Julie Lythcott-Haims in her book *How to Raise an Adult,* "Kids with overinvolved parents and rigidly structured childhoods suffer psychological blowback in college."[23] Some evidence bears this out: A 2011 study from University of Tennessee at Chattanooga found that students with "hovering" or "helicopter" parents were more likely to take medication for anxiety, depression or both.

On the other side of the debate, James Emery White (among others) argues that "one of the marks of Generation Z is that they are being raised, by and large, by Generation X—a generation that was warned repeatedly not to become 'helicopter' parents. . . . As a result, Generation Z is very self-directed."[24] He sees Millennials as having been raised by overprotective (Boomer) parents, but Gen Z by *under*protective (Gen X) parents. Gen X, White believes, would rather err on the side of being too loose than too strict. But the problem is that, in an age of social media, ubiquitous porn, self-harm, cyberbullying and sexting, children need greater protection than ever before—not less. Thanks to their parents, however, Gen Z is growing up too fast, and childhood has slowly evaporated in the name of independence and freedom. Instead of being formed and disciplined by their parents, screenagers are increasingly shaped by the media. (This is especially true of pornography, which is shaping sexual norms and expectations in radical ways.) If the teens in Barna's research are to be believed, many don't have much (if any) parental oversight of their Wi-Fi-enabled activities. The problems unique to Gen Z, White and others say, can be laid at the feet of hands-off parenting.

But what if both concerns are valid? Might it be true that Gen Z's parents are overinvolved in many of the wrong ways and too detached in others?

We might call this "double-minded parenting"—an approach that is wrongside-out if the goal is to raise resilient, emotionally intelligent adults.

Gen Z's parents may be overinvolved in many of the wrong ways and too detached in others

These are the six trends Barna has identified that are powerfully at work to create the ethos of the next generation:

1. They are screenagers.

2. Their worldview is post-Christian.

3. "Safe spaces" are normal.

4. Real safety is a myth.

5. They are diverse.

6. Their parents are double-minded.

Under these influences, who is Gen Z becoming? Let's look more closely at who they are and what's most important to them.

My Identity & My Life Goals

What's the relationship between how teens see themselves now and their hopes for the future? We asked 13- to 18-year-olds what aspects of identity are most important to them today, and what accomplishments are a priority for them to achieve before age 30. Here's a look at what defines Gen Z now and what they hope will define them as they emerge fully into adulthood.

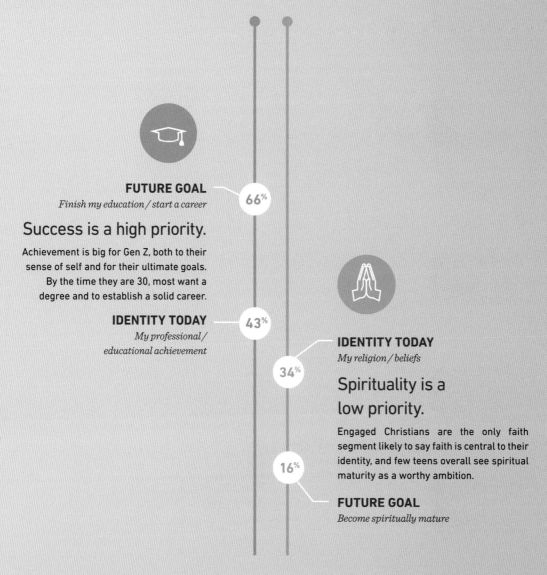

FUTURE GOAL

Finish my education / start a career

66%

Success is a high priority.

Achievement is big for Gen Z, both to their sense of self and for their ultimate goals. By the time they are 30, most want a degree and to establish a solid career.

IDENTITY TODAY

My professional / educational achievement

43%

IDENTITY TODAY

My religion / beliefs

34%

Spirituality is a low priority.

Engaged Christians are the only faith segment likely to say faith is central to their identity, and few teens overall see spiritual maturity as a worthy ambition.

16%

FUTURE GOAL

Become spiritually mature

U.S. adults ages 19 and older, *n*=1,517, Nov. 4–16, 2016. Teens ages 13–18, *n*=1,490, Nov. 4–16, 2016. Teens, ages 13-18, *n*=507, July 7–18, 2017.

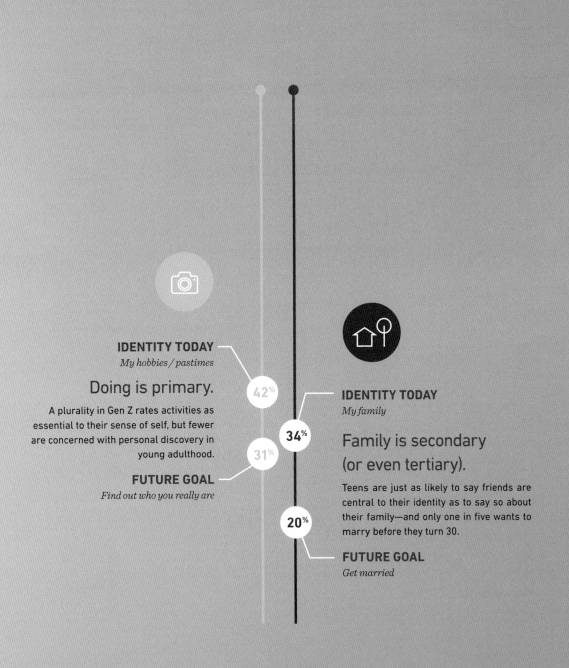

IDENTITY TODAY
My hobbies / pastimes

Doing is primary.

A plurality in Gen Z rates activities as essential to their sense of self, but fewer are concerned with personal discovery in young adulthood.

FUTURE GOAL
Find out who you really are

42%

31%

IDENTITY TODAY
My family

Family is secondary (or even tertiary).

Teens are just as likely to say friends are central to their identity as to say so about their family—and only one in five wants to marry before they turn 30.

FUTURE GOAL
Get married

34%

20%

 **AT A GLANCE** |—

A plurality of Gen Z considers personal achievement (43%) and hobbies (42%) most important to their sense of self.

All other generations rank family at the top of the list.

Only one-third of teens believes lying is wrong (34%),

compared to three out of five Elders (61%), the oldest adult generation.

One in eight describes their sexual orientation as something other than heterosexual (12%).

Those who identify as bisexual make up more than half of that proportion (7%).

Seven out of 10 believe it's acceptable to be born one gender and feel like another (69%).

Three in 10 teens report personally knowing someone, most often a peer, who has changed his or her gender identity.

Two-thirds want to finish their education (66%), start a career (66%) and become financially independent (65%) by age 30.

Only one in five wants to get married by then (20%).

2

Who I Am & What Matters Most

What traits, preferences and self-perceptions make Gen Z who they are?

Personal achievement, whether educational or professional, and hobbies and pastimes are most central to Gen Z's identity. Twice as many teens as Boomers strongly agree that these are important to their sense of self, while older adults are more likely to say their family background and religion are central to their identity (one in three in Gen Z considers these important).

My ———— Is Very Important to My Sense of Self

● Gen Z   ● Gen X
● Millennials   ● Boomers

	Professional / educational achievement	Hobbies / pastimes	Gender / sexuality	Group of friends	Family background / upbringing	Religion / religious beliefs	Race / ethnicity	Region I'm from	Social / economic class	Political affiliation
Gen Z	43%	42%	37%	35%	34%	34%	23%	21%	13%	13%
Millennials	35%	35%	31%	27%	40%	32%	22%	27%	15%	18%
Gen X	21%	28%	28%	19%	40%	34%	22%	20%	12%	14%
Boomers	22%	23%	33%	22%	46%	43%	23%	23%	13%	13%

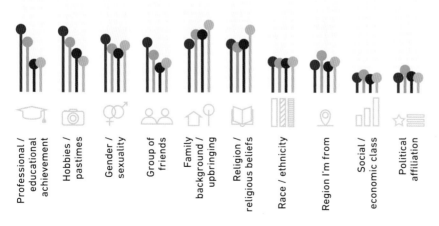

U.S. teens ages 13–18, n=1,490, Nov. 4–16, 2016. U.S. adults 19 and older, n=1,517, Nov. 4–16, 2016.

The move away from identification with religious beliefs is a widespread cultural phenomenon, as we examined in chapter 1, but the comparative indifference of Gen Z to their upbringing or family background is likewise notable (and also somewhat dissonant—when researchers ask teens who they most look up to as a role model, half say their parents and one in seven says another family member). It's not yet clear if this refocusing of identity away from family is the continuation of a descending generational trend, or if Gen Z will gain a deeper appreciation for the influence of their family of origin as they leave the nest. Time will tell.

There are significant differences when we look at teens by ethnicity. First, and not surprisingly, Gen Z racial minorities are substantially more likely than whites to consider their race or ethnicity important to their sense of self. African Americans feel most strongly about this—half strongly agree

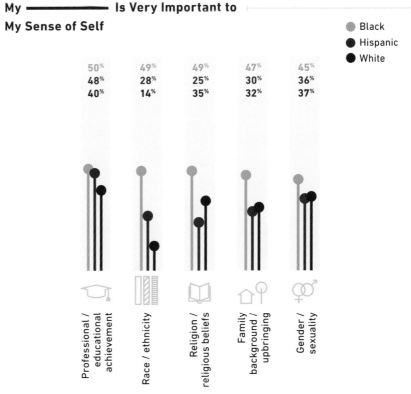

My ——————— Is Very Important to My Sense of Self

- Black
- Hispanic
- White

	Professional / educational achievement	Race / ethnicity	Religion / religious beliefs	Family background / upbringing	Gender / sexuality
Black	50%	49%	49%	47%	45%
Hispanic	48%	28%	25%	30%	36%
White	40%	14%	35%	32%	37%

U.S. teens ages 13–18, n=1,490, Nov. 4–16, 2016.

compared to only one in seven white teens—and Latino / Hispanic teens fall in between. Black teenagers are also more likely than white youth to consider their family background, achievement, religious beliefs and gender or sexuality important to their identity. Hispanic teens are likewise more apt to rate achievement as important, but they are *least* likely to strongly agree that religion plays a significant role in their sense of self.

Researchers also find sizable differences when they look at Gen Z faith groups. Engaged Christians are much more likely than average to consider their religious beliefs (and, to a lesser extent, achievement and family background) very important to their identity. The one-third of teens with no religious affiliation is, by contrast, far less likely to say that religion (12%) or family (22%) are significant factors when it comes to their sense of self.

Engaged Christians are much more likely than average to consider their religious beliefs very important to their identity

My ———— Is Very Important to My Sense of Self

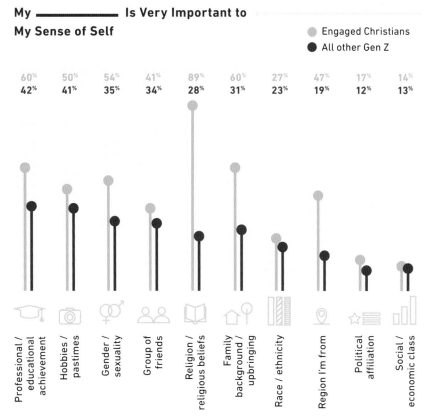

- Engaged Christians
- All other Gen Z

	Professional / educational achievement	Hobbies / pastimes	Gender / sexuality	Group of friends	Religion / religious beliefs	Family background / upbringing	Race / ethnicity	Region I'm from	Political affiliation	Social / economic class
Engaged Christians	60%	50%	54%	41%	89%	60%	27%	47%	17%	14%
All other Gen Z	42%	41%	35%	34%	28%	31%	23%	19%	12%	13%

U.S. teens ages 13–18, *n*=1,490. Nov. 4–16, 2016.

(Continued on page 46)

Q & A W I T H
J O H N A. M U R R A Y

HEAD OF CENTRAL CHRISTIAN SCHOOL

John serves as Head of Central Christian School in St. Louis, Missouri, a 2016 National Blue Ribbon School. He is also Founder and Director of Central Leadership Forum and serves as President of the Christian Schools Association of St. Louis. His award-winning articles on education, history, media and youth culture have appeared in numerous publications, including *The Wall Street Journal, USA Today, The St. Louis Post-Dispatch* and FoxNews. com. His new book is *In Whose Image? Image-Bearers of God vs. the Image-Makers of Our Time.* John and his wife, Barbara, are parents of four Gen Z children.

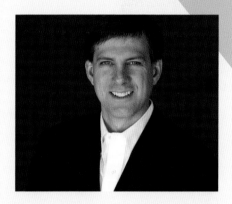

Barna has been asking people about their sense of identity for a number of years now. A plurality in each adult generation identifies their family background as very important to their sense of self, but Gen Z is much less likely to do so—and more likely to rate personal achievement, hobbies, their gender or sexuality, and their friends as essential. What role do you see for educators and mentors in coaching youth in the process of identity formation?

As George Barna has shown, a person's worldview is most often in place by the time they reach the age of 13. In light of this research, over the past six years I have developed the first part of a textbook for eighth-grade

students around six questions to help them better understand themselves and others as God's image-bearers. These questions speak to what Gen Z is identifying as important to their sense of self—and give Christian educators a segue to help teens explore what it means to be an image-bearer of God.

Who am I? To be made in the image of God means we are set apart from the rest of creation, "a little lower than the angels," as King David wrote in Psalm 8. David praises God for His creation: "For you created my inmost being; you knit me together in my mother's womb. I praise you because I am fearfully and wonderfully made." Grasping this biblical perspective helps students see their essential worth in a new light.

How does the media influence me? Given the amount of media teens are exposed to by the time they turn 18, Christian educators must also help students comprehend 1) how it influences them, 2) what their vulnerabilities are and 3) how to discern the worldviews behind the media. By equipping students to recognize the impact of media on brain development in particular, they can see firsthand how critical it is to guard their hearts and minds against harmful influences and resist being conformed to the pattern of this world (see Rom. 12).

What is my identity? Within the framework of viewing ourselves and others as image-bearers, Christian educators can help students examine different aspects of their identity—including race, gender, social status and body image (see Gal. 3:28)—through a healthy, biblical worldview. When students see their physical selves as God's masterpieces (see Eph. 2:10), they see themselves as God sees them. Ultimately this allows them to pursue their place and purpose in society, having an others-centered orientation and developing a genuine concern for the poor and disenfranchised.

Where did I come from? Christian educators must play a key role in demonstrating how faith and science are not mutually exclusive. Acknowledging that God created the heavens and the earth, and us as His image-bearers, Christian educators can reinforce and encourage students' faith through the areas of science that point to an intelligent, purposeful Creator. The hundreds of factors necessary for Earth to support life and the complexities of our bodies as God's image-bearers greatly diminish the idea that we are accidental side effects of a massive explosion.

Where does my creativity come from? Christian educators can also expose their students to the origin of communication and the arts—particularly as they reflect the image and creativity of God. By understanding how we bear God's image through our ability to create and communicate, students can use their gifts and talents to glorify God. Interestingly, many of the artistic and innovative geniuses through history gave God the glory for their work—from literature to the fine arts, from the printing press to the telegraph to motion pictures—which encourages students to use their abilities to be culture-makers, not just consumers.

How should I view others? Self-worth crumbles when we view others or ourselves as less than we are in God's eyes. To help students fathom the devastating effects of passive-aggressive, sexual and mean-spirited social media, and the significance of not viewing others as image-bearers, educators must give them a framework to be loving, kind, gentle, forgiving and others-centered—nurturing them to be much-needed culture-change agents in their generation.

Sexuality & Gender

Gen Z, more than older generations, considers their sexuality or gender to be central to their sense of personal identity. Of course, some life-stage effects are likely at work; teens whose physiological sexuality is developing are naturally more attuned to sexuality in general. Yet the fact that this appears to be so important, and that public debate surrounding sexuality and gender is so culturally pervasive, strongly suggests these topics will be a central theme for Gen Z as they move into adulthood. Ideas and experiences teens are dealing with now will undoubtedly shape their perspectives in the future.

It's interesting that engaged Christians, even more than other young people, consider their gender or sexuality as central to their sense of self. It's likely this is due to the ubiquity of the topic in the wider culture—for example, the entire January 2017 issue of *National Geographic* was dedicated to the subject, and "bathroom wars" have been much in the news—and churches' efforts to respond faithfully through conversation and biblical education.

About one in eight of all 13- to 18-year-olds describes their sexual orientation as something other than heterosexual or straight (12%), with those who identify as bisexual making up more than half of that proportion (7%). (To put that in context, for as long as Barna has asked survey respondents about their sexual orientation, about 3 percent of all U.S. adults have identified as LGBT.) Faith identity and practice correlate with a higher tendency to identify as straight, with nearly all engaged Christians (99%) saying they are heterosexual (vs. 86% all Gen Z). On the other hand, teens with no religious affiliation are less likely than others to describe themselves as straight (79%; 13% consider themselves bisexual).

In focus groups with 13- to 18-year-olds, the subject of gender, in particular, often came up in conversation, leading researchers to supplement the original surveys with further quantitative interviews on the topic. They found that only half of today's teens believe one's sex at birth defines one's gender. One-third says gender is "what a person feels like." Twelve percent do not know how to answer this question, while smaller percentages say "a person's desires or sexual attraction" or "the way society sees a person."

Faith is a guide to perspectives on gender, but there are still many Christian teens who don't necessarily connect gender with birth sex. Three-quarters of engaged Christians say one's gender is the sex a person was born

Gen Z, more than older generations, considers their sexuality or gender to be central to their sense of self

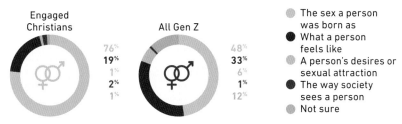

Gender Is Primarily Based on . . .

Engaged Christians

- 76%
- 19%
- 1%
- 2%
- 1%

All Gen Z

- 48%
- 33%
- 6%
- 1%
- 12%

- The sex a person was born as
- What a person feels like
- A person's desires or sexual attraction
- The way society sees a person
- Not sure

U.S. teens ages 13–18, *n*=485, July 7–18, 2017.

with; one in five says it's what a person feels like (19%). But views are more mixed among churched Christians who do not qualify as engaged: One-quarter says a person's feelings are the primary basis of gender (27%) and just over half that birth sex is the primary determinant (56%). The disparity between engaged and churched Christian teens indicates a lack of clarity about traditional Christian teaching on gender—and the growing cultural influence of the religiously unaffiliated surely plays a role in the confusion. Two in five of those with no faith believe one's gender is based on one's feelings (41%), while just one-third says a person's sex at birth is primary (35%); one in 10 says sexual attraction is the primary driver (10%).

Seven out of 10 teens think it's *definitely* or *probably* acceptable to be born one gender and feel like another. (In fact, three in 10 report personally knowing someone, most often a peer, who has changed his or her gender identity.) About one in 10 young people is not sure it's acceptable for someone to feel a different gender from their birth sex. Among engaged Christians, about one in six says they are not sure (17%), while the rest are split between those who believe it is acceptable (44%) and those who say it is *not* (40%).

If focus group participants are reflective of the broader Gen Z population, their evolving and sometimes contradictory views are often grounded in a desire to express solidarity with marginalized groups like transgender people. Gender issues, like a number of others they face, leave many teens feeling both compassion and confusion.

How teens would feel about, and what they would say to, a peer who was questioning or considering changing their gender also reveal a lot about their opinions on the topic. Nearly half of Gen Z say they would feel neutral if a

It Is Acceptable for Someone to Be Born One Gender and Feel Like Another

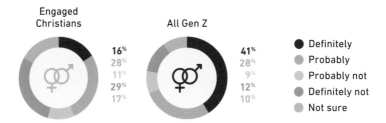

Engaged Christians

16%
28%
11%
29%
17%

All Gen Z

41%
28%
9%
12%
10%

● Definitely
◐ Probably
○ Probably not
◑ Definitely not
◔ Not sure

U.S. teens ages 13–18, n=485, July 7–18, 2017.

friend was questioning their gender (45%) and about one in three would feel concerned (31%). One in nine says they would be "happy for them" (11%) and 14 percent are not sure. Young women are more likely to say they would be happy (14% vs. 5% young men).

Their own feelings aside, most teens would either remain neutral (38%) or encourage a friend (31%) who was considering a gender change; few would actively discourage it (8%). Again, the percentage on the positive end of responses is greater among young women than among young men. And teen girls are also more likely to say it is definitely okay for someone to "physically change their body (through hormones or surgery) to become another gender" (24% vs. 10% teen boys). Combined, about two in five teens believe it is okay (42%) for someone to change their body to become a gender other than their

It Is OK for Someone to Change Their Body to Become Another Gender

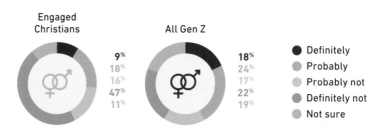

Engaged Christians

9%
18%
16%
47%
11%

All Gen Z

18%
24%
17%
22%
19%

● Definitely
◐ Probably
○ Probably not
◑ Definitely not
◔ Not sure

U.S. teens ages 13–18, n=485, July 7–18, 2017.

birth sex, and a similar proportion says doing so is not okay (39%). One in five is just not sure.

When it comes to faith groups, about the same percentage of engaged Christians would discourage a friend's plans to change their gender (24%) as would encourage such a change (21%)—but even so, many would do neither (40%). Considering their own feelings, engaged Christians are more likely than teens with no religious affiliation to be concerned for a friend who wants to change their gender (53% vs. 24%). Interestingly, those with no faith are not more likely to be "happy" for a friend; rather, they are more likely to be neutral (56% vs. 27% engaged Christians). Regarding physical alterations, engaged Christians are most likely to believe this is not okay (63%), compared with half of churched Christians (51%), one in three unchurched Christians (34%) and one in four teens with no religious faith (28%).

Whatever their opinions or experiences, half of all Gen Z think gender is talked about too much in today's society. However, teens are more likely to say gender is discussed among their peers "just the right amount."

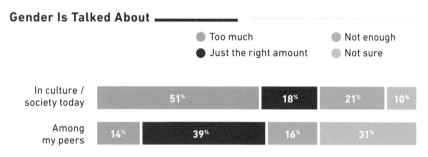

Gender Is Talked About

- ⬤ Too much
- ⬤ Just the right amount
- ⬤ Not enough
- ⬤ Not sure

In culture / society today	51%	18%	21%	10%
Among my peers	14%	39%	16%	31%

U.S. teens ages 13–18, *n*=485, July 7–18, 2017.

Friends & Neighbors

Who are Gen Z's peers and friends? Not surprisingly, the vast majority of teens say most of their friends are from school (86%), followed far behind by school-based extracurriculars (31%), athletic teams (25%) and their local neighborhood (24%); only one in five says their friends are mostly from church. Not surprisingly, engaged Christians (66%) and churched teens (31%) are more likely than others to say church is largely where their friendships are based.

Within their peer groups, Gen Z reports a mix of homogeneity and diversity. Homogeneity is more common in small towns and rural areas, while diversity is more the rule in larger cities. One way to assess the experience of diversity is whether a teenager shares his beliefs in common with most of his friends; Gen Z is split into nearly even thirds on this question—though racial minorities tend to be more unsure about their friends' beliefs (40% not sure vs. 28% white teens).

Most of My Friends Do Not Share My Beliefs

9% Agree strongly
22% Agree somewhat
34% Not sure
25% Disagree somewhat
10% Disagree strongly

U.S. teens ages 13–18, *n*=1,490, Nov. 4–16, 2016.

Teens (39%), along with young adult Millennials (44%), are more likely than older adults (especially Boomers, 26%) to say they often interact with people "who do not share or do not understand important parts of my identity." This is partly a function of demographics; Gen Z and Millennials are more ethnically and culturally diverse than the generations before them. But their demographic diversity also appears to drive an expectation that those around them will have different identities and beliefs—and that those differences can be a source of joy: Teens (18%) and young adults (22%) are also more likely than older adults (14%) to strongly agree that they enjoy spending time with people who are different from them. Gen Z and Millennials have a greater appreciation for integration, in practice, compared with the generations before them.

White and black teens are more likely than Hispanic young people to report often interacting with people different from them (43% white, 38% black vs. 29% Hispanic teens). Yet black teenagers are most likely to strongly agree that they enjoy spending time with people who are different from them (28% vs. 15% white, 21% Hispanic teens). So even though Gen Z is demographically

Gen Z's demographic diversity appears to drive an expectation that those around them have different identities and beliefs

diverse compared to other generations, not all teens are completely at home in that diversity.

Goals & Priorities

What aspirations are shaping Gen Z's future? Where are they headed and why?

Many in Gen Z are not yet clear about their mid-range goals (which is understandable, especially for younger teens). A plurality agrees only *somewhat* that "I have clear goals for where I want to be in five years," and one-quarter disagrees.

I Have Clear Goals for Where I Want to Be in Five Years

30% Agree strongly
42% Agree somewhat
27% Disagree strongly

U.S. teens ages 13–18, *n*=507, July 7–18, 2017.

Engaged Christians appear to have greater clarity about the next five years compared to other faith segments (45% strongly agree vs. 32% other Christians, 27% no faith). This may be because they prioritize different factors as they consider the future. As the table shows, more than half say their faith is their top priority, compared to the majority of other groups who prioritize either their personal interests or money. As Donna Freitas's work reveals, these priorities align with an overall pursuit of happiness, which nearly half of Gen Z equate with "success." (See pp. 21 for more on happiness.)

Young women tend to have a clearer vision, at least for their near future, than young men: 36 percent of teen girls *strongly* agree they have clear goals for the next five years, compared to 27 percent of teen boys. This corresponds to other evidence that young Gen Z males, like their Millennial counterparts, often lack a sense of purpose. As we saw in chapter 1, more women than

Most Important Factor When I Think About My Future

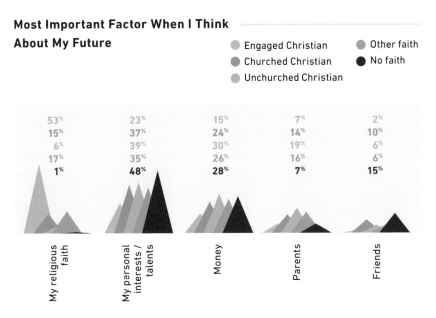

Legend:
- Engaged Christian
- Churched Christian
- Unchurched Christian
- Other faith
- No faith

	My religious faith	My personal interests / talents	Money	Parents	Friends
Engaged Christian	53%	23%	15%	7%	2%
Churched Christian	15%	37%	24%	14%	10%
Unchurched Christian	6%	39%	30%	19%	6%
Other faith	17%	35%	26%	16%	6%
No faith	1%	48%	28%	7%	15%

U.S. teens ages 13–18, *n*=1,490, Nov. 4–16, 2016.

men enroll in college each year. And according to the U.S. Bureau of Labor Statistics, male unemployment is consistently higher than female unemployment across the board, but especially among young adults (8.6% men ages 20–24, 6.3% women ages 20–24).[25] Young men are less likely than young women to be in college or to be working. No wonder many of them are feeling aimless and at sea.

Looking beyond the mid-term, there also are mixed feelings about growing up. Half are *somewhat* excited about becoming an adult (52%), while one in four is not looking forward to it (28%). Interestingly, white teens—who tend to enjoy greater wealth and comfort, on average—are more likely than black and Hispanic young people to say they are not excited to grow up (32% vs. 15% black teens, 26% Hispanic teens).

We see another symptom of a reluctance to embrace independence in the dramatic drop-off in teen driving: Nearly all Boomers had their driver's license by their senior year of high school, but more than one in four of today's seniors is not licensed to drive.[26]

Just one in five among all Gen Z youth is enthusiastic about the advent of adulthood (20%)—and these are concentrated at the more religious end of the faith spectrum: 40 percent of engaged Christians are very excited about becoming an adult, compared to 16 percent of those with no faith. It may be that more engaged Christians have a clear picture of what adulthood will mean for them, while those without a faith background lack clear expectations for who they will be and what they will do when they are on their own.

Only one in four teens says they are most looking forward to the freedoms of adulthood (22%); the other three out of four are about evenly split between those most looking forward to the responsibilities of adulthood (37%) and those who look forward to both freedoms and responsibilities (41%).

Analysts believe the generational apathy toward growing up is more evidence of a creeping lack of purpose and meaning, which comes even more sharply into focus when we look at what teens say they want to accomplish before age 30. Barna offered the same list of options to Millennials in 2013; below are both generations' answers presented side by side, for comparison:

Generational apathy is evidence of a creeping lack of purpose and meaning

I Want to Accomplish ━━━━━ Before Age 30

Gen Z		Rank		Millennials
Finish my education	66%	1	59%	Become financially independent
Start a career	66%	2	52%	Finish my education
Become financially independent	65%	3	51%	Start a career
Follow my dreams	55%	4	40%	Find out who you really are
Enjoy life before you have the responsibilities of being an adult	38%	5	31%	Follow my dreams
Find out who you really are	31%	6	29%	Become more mature spiritually
Travel to other countries	21%	7	28%	Get married
Get married	20%	8	24%	Enjoy life before you have the responsibilities of being an adult
Become more mature spiritually	16%	9	21%	Become a parent
Become a parent	12%	10	20%	Travel to other countries
Care for the poor and needy	9%	11	9%	Care for the poor and needy
Try to become famous or influential	9%	12	5%	Try to become famous or influential

U.S. teens ages 13–18, *n*=1,490, Nov. 4–16, 2016. U.S. adults 18–29, *n*=1,000, June 25–July 1, 2013.

As you can see, the trends Barna identified among Millennials—high priority on career achievement, low priority on personal and relational growth—are amplified in Gen Z. Fewer teens are interested in starting a family or becoming more spiritually mature. Nearly two out of five want to spend their 20s enjoying life before they take on the responsibilities of being adult— significantly higher than the one-quarter of Millennials who said this.

More than half of teens want to follow their dreams, yet just three in 10 want to find out who they really are. But the faith segmentation on these statements is interesting. Teens with no religious affiliation are much more likely than engaged Christians to want *both* to follow their dreams (62% vs. 42%) and to find out who they really are (41% vs. 25%). This may indicate an impulse in those with no faith to seek greater meaning.

Engaged Christians, as we might expect, are more likely to say spiritual maturity is a goal (46%) and a bit more likely to say they'd like to get married (29%) and have children (16%) before age 30. Yet these low percentages suggest the cultural tide against marriage—or at least toward delaying it—is tugging at faithful Christians, as well. Perhaps many teens consider marriage and parenting to be "adult responsibilities" that they are planning to avoid during their 20s.

The Primary Mark of Adulthood: Gen Z vs. Millennials

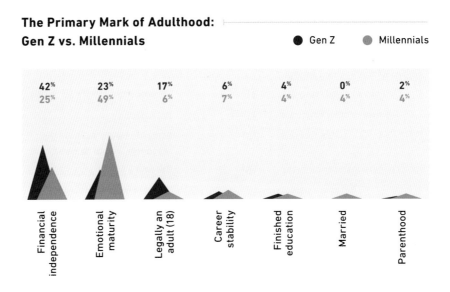

● Gen Z ● Millennials

	Financial independence	Emotional maturity	Legally an adult (18)	Career stability	Finished education	Married	Parenthood
Gen Z	42%	23%	17%	6%	4%	0%	2%
Millennials	25%	49%	6%	7%	4%	4%	4%

U.S. teens ages 13–18, n=1,490, Nov. 4–16, 2016. U.S. adults 18–29, n=563, June 25–July 1, 2013.

How will they know when they have "arrived" at adulthood? Barna also asked this question among Millennials in 2013—and the differences are stark. Financial independence looms large for many teens in a way it did not for 18- to 29-year-old Millennials; doubtless the country's (and their parents') financial problems since the Great Recession are a big influence here. Emotional maturity, on the other hand—of such supreme importance to many Millennial twentysomethings—is significant to fewer than one in four teenagers. (And notice that marriage—a key marker of adulthood just a few generations ago—doesn't even make their list.) It will be interesting to see if these priorities shift as Gen Z moves into adulthood.

The people teens look up to—and the reasons why—are another window into their ultimate goals. As noted earlier, a sizable majority of Gen Z says their parents or another family member is their role model. But why? On an open-ended question, among the top 10 answers is that the role model is hardworking and responsible, that he or she provides for their family, that they have a good career, that they have an education, that they are successful and that he or she is independent. To be clear: Six out of the top 10 reasons teens look up to their role model are related to career or financial success.

Morality & Values

Moral relativism is taking deeper root in America. One-quarter of Gen Z strongly agrees that what is morally right and wrong changes over time based on society, and they are nearly on par with Millennials in believing each individual is his or her own moral arbiter.

Beliefs About Morality, by Generation

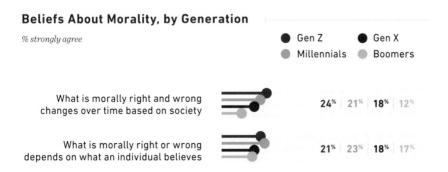

% strongly agree

● Gen Z   ● Gen X
● Millennials   ○ Boomers

What is morally right and wrong changes over time based on society   24% | 21% | 18% | 12%

What is morally right or wrong depends on what an individual believes   21% | 23% | 18% | 17%

U.S. teens ages 13–18, *n*=1,490, Nov. 4–16, 2016. U.S. adults 19 and older, *n*=1,517, Nov. 4–16, 2016

Teens in Barna focus groups elaborated on their perspective. One participant said, "Society changes and what's good or bad changes, as well. It is all relative to what's happening in the world." What they likely haven't heard as much of is that there exists an objective morality, compared to which all human morality falls short. At their best, our redefinitions over time are not according to whim but in an effort to get closer to true morality.

Beliefs About Moral Issues, by Generation

% strongly agree

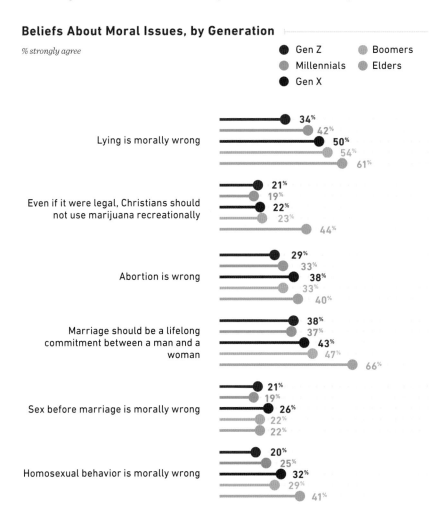

● Gen Z   ● Boomers
● Millennials   ● Elders
● Gen X

Lying is morally wrong
- 34%
- 42%
- 50%
- 54%
- 61%

Even if it were legal, Christians should not use marijuana recreationally
- 21%
- 19%
- 22%
- 23%
- 44%

Abortion is wrong
- 29%
- 33%
- 38%
- 33%
- 40%

Marriage should be a lifelong commitment between a man and a woman
- 38%
- 37%
- 43%
- 47%
- 66%

Sex before marriage is morally wrong
- 21%
- 19%
- 26%
- 22%
- 22%

Homosexual behavior is morally wrong
- 20%
- 25%
- 32%
- 29%
- 41%

U.S. teens ages 13–18, *n*=1,490, Nov. 4–16, 2016. U.S. adults 19 and older, *n*=1,517, Nov. 4–16, 2016

Looking at some basic moral principles, there is a clear generational decline in the moral compass of Americans. (Elders are a shrinking proportion of the overall population, but are included here for perspective.) Fully three out of five among the eldest generation strongly agree that lying is immoral, while only one-third of Gen Z believes lying is wrong; there is a continuous slide by generation in conviction about this moral principle. Generational

Looking at basic moral principles, there is a clear generational decline in the nation's moral compass

Beliefs About Moral Issues, by Faith Segment

% strongly agree

Engaged Christian
Churched Christian
Unchurched Christian
Other faith
No faith

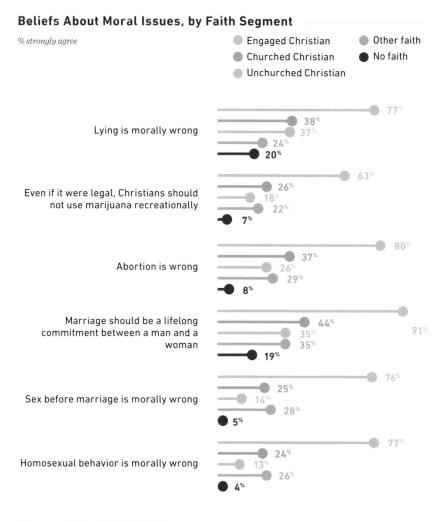

Lying is morally wrong
77%
38%
37%
24%
20%

Even if it were legal, Christians should not use marijuana recreationally
63%
26%
18%
22%
7%

Abortion is wrong
80%
37%
26%
29%
8%

Marriage should be a lifelong commitment between a man and a woman
91%
44%
35%
35%
19%

Sex before marriage is morally wrong
76%
25%
14%
28%
5%

Homosexual behavior is morally wrong
77%
24%
13%
26%
4%

U.S. teens ages 13–18, *n*=1,490, Nov. 4–16, 2016.

perspectives on abortion, use of recreational drugs and sex before marriage are more similar, yet Gen Z is also least likely to consider abortion wrong.

Overall Gen Z holds the most liberal views when it comes to issues of sexuality. They are least likely to agree that marriage should be a lifelong commitment between a man and a woman (tied with Millennials) and to have moral objections to same-sex sexual activity.

Some culture watchers have suggested that Gen Z is "more conservative" than their predecessors, but Barna researchers see little evidence of this claim. Moral shifts that began during the sexual revolution of the 1960s have made an indelible cultural impact, with today's teens the most liberal generation thus far. (There is some anecdotal evidence that Gen Z overall may have more conservative economic views than Millennials, but socially speaking, they tend to be just as, if not more, liberal than their predecessors.)

Engaged Christian teens, however, are a stark contrast to their peers on moral issues. We see significant gaps between their beliefs and all others, including other churchgoing teens, on most moral issues, suggesting that church attendance alone does not create distinctive believers. Instead, only those teens who grow up with strong Christian education and intentional discipleship are taking the Bible's moral principles to heart, while others look more like the broader culture. One churchgoing teen from the focus groups is a clear example: "I believe in God, in a higher power, I believe in Jesus. But I don't believe you necessarily have to follow the Bible step-by-step. I believe that if you're an overall good person and you have good intentions, that's all you need."

Gen Z, including engaged Christians, are generally opposed to challenging others' beliefs. They part ways with other teens, however, when it comes to evaluating the reliability of their own beliefs in light of how those beliefs might affect others. Engaged Christian teens *and* adults are twice as likely as their peers to strongly *disagree* that "if your beliefs offend someone or hurt their feelings, they are probably wrong." That is, two-thirds do not equate the truth of their beliefs with how appealing (or unappealing) they are to others.

> Church attendance alone does not create distinctive believers

z

Taken together, and considered in light of the trends examined in chapter 1, these data sketch a portrait of a generation that feels at once ambivalent about the present and apprehensive about the future. Many seem to believe that what I do is who I am—a self based on personal achievement and risk mitigation, in a world where so many things are up for grabs. Barna analysts believe many teens are disempowered and disengaged, entertained but not inspired. They are hyperaware of their public image—according to Freitas, eight out of 10 agree "I'm aware that my name is a brand and that I need to cultivate it carefully"[27]—but few feel truly known.

And many don't want to rock the boat. Adding to their uncertainty is growing cultural (and generational) ambiguity surrounding morality, the basic human framework for understanding what it means to be a good person and to live a good life.

So what happens when their uncertainty and ambiguity cross paths with the historic Christian faith?

A Love / Hate Relationship with Church

Not all teens want to be in church. Most of those who say church is not important to them still consider themselves Christian, but some don't actually believe in God—about one in five churchgoers in this study says they are atheist, agnostic or none. Some in Gen Z attend solely because their parents require it, but at least a few are in church by choice. So why do some like church and some hate it? Barna looked at engaged Christians compared with all other churched teens.

Is Attending Church Important to You?

Engaged Christians

79%
19%
2%

Churchgoers
(not engaged)

25%
42%
28%
5%

● Very important
● Somewhat important
○ Not too important
● Not at all important

Pros & Cons

What is it that teens like and don't like about church? Here is a comparison of churchgoing teens with engaged Christians when it comes to their perceptions of church.

● **Engaged Christians**
● **Churchgoers** *(not engaged)*

Positive *% yes*

On the positive side of the ledger churchgoing teens perceive their church to be tolerant, personally relevant, and a place where they can be authentically themselves.

❝ The church is a place to find answers to live a meaningful life.   95%   77%

❝ I feel like I can 'be myself' at church.   94%   71%

❝ The church is relevant for my life.   90%   79%

❝ The people at church are tolerant of those with different beliefs.   64%   63%

Negative *% yes*

On the negative side, many perceive church to be anti-science, overprotective, filled with hypocrites and unsafe place to express doubt.

❝ The church seems to reject much of what science tells us about the world.   37%   53%

❝ The church is overprotective of teenagers.   28%   41%

❝ The people at church are hypocritical.   21%   42%

❝ The church is not a safe place to express doubts.   12%   32%

Teens ages 13–18, *n*=507, July 7–18, 2017.

Z AT A GLANCE

Three in 10 non-Christian teens say the problem of evil is a barrier to faith (29%).

Christians' hypocrisy and the conflict between science and scripture are other common hurdles.

Only about one in four among all Gen Z believes science and the Bible are complementary (28%),

compared to almost half of Boomers (45%) and more than one-third of Gen X (36%).

Four out of five churchgoing teens say church is relevant to them (82%).

The same proportion agrees church is a good place to find answers to live a meaningful life (82%).

Three out of five Christians who don't think church is important say "I find God elsewhere" (61%).

Non-Christians who avoid church are more likely to say it's "not relevant to me" (64%).

One out of five teens chooses a negative, judgmental image to represent a Christian church (21%).

One in three opts for a cross, which is emotionally more neutral (35%).

3

Faith, Truth & Church

Faith

As we saw in chapter 1, the cultural pressure to identify as Christian has lifted over the past two decades—a phenomenon seen most dramatically in Gen Z's religious self-identification (or growing lack thereof). "Atheist" is no longer a bad word: The percentage of teens who identify as such is double that of

Non-Christians' Barriers to Faith

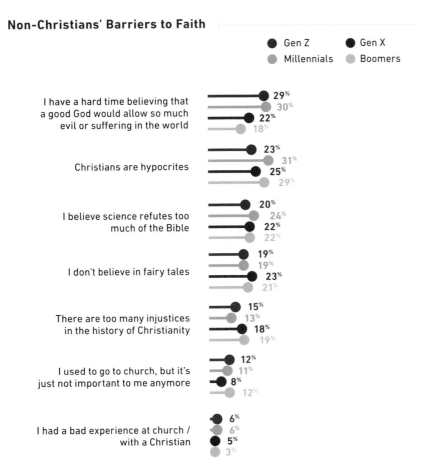

● Gen Z ● Gen X
● Millennials ● Boomers

I have a hard time believing that a good God would allow so much evil or suffering in the world
- 29%
- 30%
- 22%
- 18%

Christians are hypocrites
- 23%
- 31%
- 25%
- 29%

I believe science refutes too much of the Bible
- 20%
- 24%
- 22%
- 22%

I don't believe in fairy tales
- 19%
- 19%
- 23%
- 21%

There are too many injustices in the history of Christianity
- 15%
- 13%
- 18%
- 19%

I used to go to church, but it's just not important to me anymore
- 12%
- 11%
- 8%
- 12%

I had a bad experience at church / with a Christian
- 6%
- 6%
- 5%
- 3%

U.S. teens ages 13–18, n=621, Nov. 4–16, 2016. U.S. adults 19 and older, n=486, Nov. 4–16, 2016.

older generations. The proportion that identifies as Christian likewise drops from generation to generation. Three out of four Boomers are Protestant or Catholic Christians (75%), while just three in five 13- to 18-year-olds say they are some kind of Christian (59%).

Looking at generational faith affiliation data (see pp. 25), one naturally wonders what has led to the precipitous falling off. Barna asked non-Christians of all ages about their biggest barriers to faith. Gen Z nonbelievers have much in common with their older counterparts in this regard, but a few differences stick out. Teens, along with young adults, are more likely than older Americans to say the problem of evil and suffering is a deal breaker for them. It appears that today's youth, like so many hurting people throughout history, struggle to find a compelling argument for the existence of both evil and a good and loving God.

Interestingly, Gen Z nonbelievers appear less likely than non-Christian adults to cite Christians' hypocrisy as a significant barrier—but just as likely to say they have personally had a bad experience with Christians or a church. On a separate but related question, teens overall were somewhat less inclined than U.S. adults to strongly agree that "religious people are judgmental" (17% vs. 24% all adults). Current political issues, especially LGBTQ rights, poverty and immigration policy, may impact whether this perception holds as Gen Z gets older.

Truth

More than one-third of Gen Z believes it is not possible to know for sure if God is real (37%), compared to 32 percent of all adults. On the other side of the coin, teens who do believe one can know God exists are less likely than adults to say they are very convinced that is true (54% vs. 64% all adults who believe in God). This demonstrates an insight that emerges time and again from analysis: For many teens, truth seems relative at best and, at worst, altogether unknowable.

Their lack of confidence is on pace with the broader culture's all-out embrace of relativism. More than half of all Americans, both teens (58%) and adults (62%), agree with the statement "Many religions can lead to eternal life; there is no 'one true religion.'" When that kind of universalism is paired with deep confusion about the nature of truth, it's impossible to assess the

> For many teens, truth seems relative at best and, at worst, altogether unknowable

"truth" of one's beliefs. As one focus group participant explained, "There is no such thing as truth, but there are facts. People can believe whatever truth they want. [There is] always room for truth to change."

There's a growing sense among Gen Z that what's true for someone else may not be "true for me"; they are much less apt than older adults (especially Boomers, 85%) to agree that "a person can be wrong about something that they sincerely believe in" (66%). For a considerable minority of teens, sincerely believing something makes it true.

At the same time some are leaning toward sincerity as a marker for truth, more are leaning hard in the other direction. Nearly half of teens, on par with Millennials, say "I need factual evidence to support my beliefs" (46%)—which helps to explain their uneasiness with the relationship between science and the Bible. Significantly fewer teens and young adults than Gen X and Boomers see the two as complementary.

One Christian focus group participant's comments capture the general uncertainty about faith and science. When asked, "Does science ever make

There is a growing sense among Gen Z that what's true for someone else may not be "true for me"

Science & the Bible Are . . .

In Conflict
I consider myself to be on the side of science.

Independent
They refer to different aspects of reality.

Complementary
Each can be used to help support the other.

In Conflict
I consider myself to be on the side of the Bible.

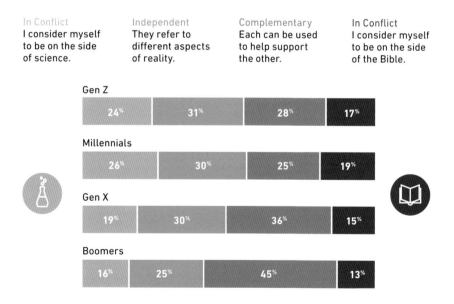

Gen Z
| 24% | 31% | 28% | 17% |

Millennials
| 26% | 30% | 25% | 19% |

Gen X
| 19% | 30% | 36% | 15% |

Boomers
| 16% | 25% | 45% | 13% |

U.S. teens ages 13–18, *n*=1,490, Nov. 4–16, 2016. U.S. adults 19 and older, *n*=1,517, Nov. 4–16, 2016.

you question your own beliefs?" he replied, "Yeah, like the stuff we're learning in school today. Not only evolution, but other theories like how the world came to be, that definitely makes you question it because they're scientists, they study this every day. In the end I'll still believe in God, but I can't totally ignore it. It's there, I learned it in school. There's nothing I can do about it."

Many teens still respect the Scriptures, but it's unclear that such reverence will last into adulthood. Barna has tracked attitudes about the Bible in the U.S. population since 2011, through the State of the Bible research with American Bible Society. For now, teens' perceptions of the Bible still tend to mirror those of their mostly Gen X parents, while Millennial twentysomethings are more skeptical. Looking at two key Bible metrics—its perceived authority and its relevance for people's lives—we find that teens and Gen X report similar beliefs and attitudes (for example, seven out of 10 believe the Bible is God's word), while Millennials are more likely to be skeptical.

The Best Definition of the Bible

% among U.S. teens and adults 13 and older

- ⬤ The actual word of God and should be taken literally, word for word
- ⬤ The inspired word of God and has no errors, although some verses are meant to be symbolic rather than literal
- ⬤ The inspired word of God but has some factual or historical errors
- ⬤ Not inspired by God but tells how the writers of the Bible understood the ways and principles of God
- ⬤ Just another book of teaching written by men that contains stories and advice
- ⬤ Other / don't know

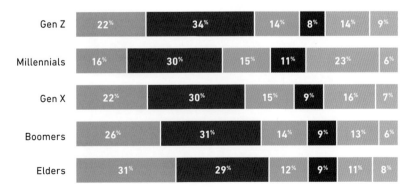

Gen Z	22%	34%	14%	8%	14%	9%
Millennials	16%	30%	15%	11%	23%	6%
Gen X	22%	30%	15%	9%	16%	7%
Boomers	26%	31%	14%	9%	13%	6%
Elders	31%	29%	12%	9%	11%	8%

U.S. teens ages 13–17, *n*=1,056, Feb. 2015. U.S. adults 18 and older, *n*=12,187, 2011–2016.

It's possible, of course, that the dropout phenomenon we see in Millennials—where young adults head off to college or strike out on their own and then experience a rise in skepticism—is unique to that generation. But, given the balance of other data that indicates less faith and more confusion about truth in Gen Z, it seems unlikely.

The Bible's Relevance

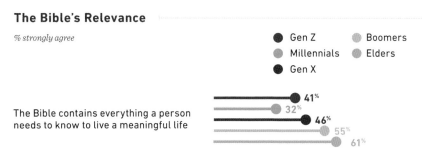

% strongly agree

● Gen Z   ● Boomers
● Millennials ● Elders
● Gen X

The Bible contains everything a person needs to know to live a meaningful life

41%
32%
46%
55%
61%

U.S. teens ages 13–17, *n*=1,056, Feb. 2015. U.S. adults 18 and older, *n*=12,187, 2011–2016.

Church

The survey presented teens with images of church-themed activities or icons and asked them which is the best representation of a Christian church. Here is how Gen Z describes the church:

Which Image Best Represents the Christian Church?

35%   21%   15%   10%

8%   7%   2%

U.S. teens ages 13–18, *n*=1,490. Nov. 4–16, 2016.

(Continued on page 70)

Q & A WITH FIKRE PRINCE

ASSOCIATE PASTOR AT EVANGEL MINISTRIES

Fikre is an associate pastor at Evangel Ministries in Detroit, Michigan, where his focus is technology development and discipleship. For 18 years he served in youth ministry at Evangel and in various groups in the region. He holds a degree in economics from Wayne State University, and has completed studies in apologetics and biblical studies at Biola University and Detroit Bible Institute. He is married to Lakeisha, and together they have five children.

Many of the data points from this study indicate confusion or ambivalence in teens when it comes to the truth. In your experience, what impact is relativism making on youth discipleship? What difference, if any, do teens' ambivalent views of truth make to the way you approach ministry?

I believe the gospel has always had an answer for relativism, but we did not think we needed it. For many years we did not teach the gospel in a way that could be translated to different cultures and experiences, because we did not think we needed to do so. For most of our history, youth have been sheltered by their parents and local communities, who acted as gatekeepers to knowledge. But now they are able to grow up just as familiar with Korean or Kenyan culture as they are with American ways of life.

So now we can begin to talk about Christ with a greater understanding of the whole world. I can teach about absolute truth and contextual truth, and youth can understand the difference. In earlier times I was limited by kids' low level of awareness of and interaction with the world outside our community, but now I get questions about turmoil in other countries or how to understand the Bible as we learn more about civilizations that predate Israel. That is exciting.

We cannot teach God as just Israel's God, or just America's God; these kids interact in global digital communities. When we show them how big God actually is, they can see how he is at work around the globe. When we teach that God knows the heart of man and that our fleshly desires are selfish and wicked—and people all over the world, no matter their faith or non-faith, struggle with that reality—they can see all people's need for him.

Let's convey the value of all people by showing kids through the pages of the Bible that each of us is made in the image of God. Let's show them how God's people have interacted with different cultures, especially in the book of Acts. As we disciple our youth, let's help them see how the salvific work of Christ translates to different cultures and backgrounds, even if this diversity is not often shown in our local congregations.

I believe part of relativism's appeal is a desire to be accepted and to accept others. When we make it seem as though God is against youth or their friends, of course they want to find ways to rationalize or explain away that idea. A lot of what comes across as ambivalence is really kids trying to make sense of what they hear, what they see, what they know of truth and love. Relativism is only dangerous to youth if the adults in their lives cannot help them uncover the flaws and outcomes of this belief. We must communicate the truth of the gospel on a more expansive playing field, so they can see God's sovereignty at work over the whole earth.

As you can see, one-third selects a cross, a relatively neutral symbol, but one in five chooses an image that strongly suggests judgment, condemnation or "Bible thumping." One in seven believes a diverse group of young people holding hands and praying is most representative of the Church, and one in 10 says so about a crowd of worshippers with their hands raised.

There are some interesting differences by ethnicity on this question. Generally, African American and Hispanic teens tend to select images that have a communal feel (and greater diversity), whereas whites are substantially more likely to pick the cross.

Images of Church, by Ethnicity

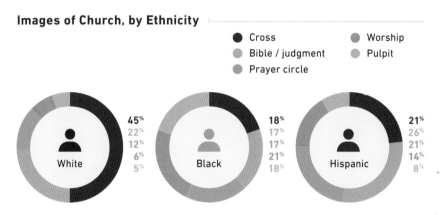

- ● Cross
- ● Bible / judgment
- ● Prayer circle
- ● Worship
- ● Pulpit

White
45%
22%
12%
6%
5%

Black
18%
17%
17%
21%
18%

Hispanic
21%
26%
21%
14%
8%

U.S. teens ages 13–18, *n*=1,490, Nov. 4–16, 2016.

Among Gen Z churchgoers (those who have attended one or more worship services within the past month), perceptions of church tend to be more positive than negative. Strong majorities of churched teens say that church "is a place to find answers to live a meaningful life" and "is relevant to my life," that "I can 'be myself' in church," and that "people at church are tolerant of those with different beliefs." Negative perceptions have significant currency, however. Half of churchgoing teens say "the church seems to reject much of what science tells us about the world" and one-third that "the church is overprotective of teenagers" or "the people at church are hypocritical." Further, one-quarter claim "the church is not a safe place to express doubts" or that the teaching they are exposed to is "rather shallow."

The positive attitudes outweigh the negatives by far. There are, however, plenty of negatives that church leaders must address—especially because

> Among Gen Z churchgoers, perceptions of church are more positive than negative

Perceptions of Church Among Churchgoing Teens

● Positive
● Negative

The church is a place to find answers to live a meaningful life
● 82%

The church is relevant for my life
● 82%

I feel like I can "be myself" at church
● 77%

The people at church are tolerant of those with different beliefs
● 63%

The church seems to reject much of what science tells us about the world
● 49%

The church is overprotective of teenagers
● 38%

The people at church are hypocritical
● 36%

The church is not a safe place to express doubts
● 27%

The faith and teachings I encounter at church seem rather shallow
● 24%

The church seems too much like an exclusive club
● 17%

U.S. churched teens ages 13–18, n=200, July 7–18, 2017.

some of these perceptions have, among Millennials, contributed to the drop-out problem in young adulthood. (See *You Lost Me* by David Kinnaman for a comprehensive look at Millennials' perceptions of church.)

More than half of Gen Z says church involvement is either "not too" (27%) or "not at all" important (27%). Only one in five says attending church is "very important" to them (20%), the least popular of the four options.

Why is church unimportant? Non-Christians and self-identified Christians have different reasons. Among those who say attending church is not important to them, three out of five Christian teens say "I find God elsewhere," while about the same proportion of non-Christians says "church is not relevant to me personally." The non-Christians' most popular answer makes sense (they're not Christians, after all), but Christians' reasoning is an indicator that at least some churches are not helping to facilitate teens' transformative connection with God.

Reasons Church Attendance Is Not Important

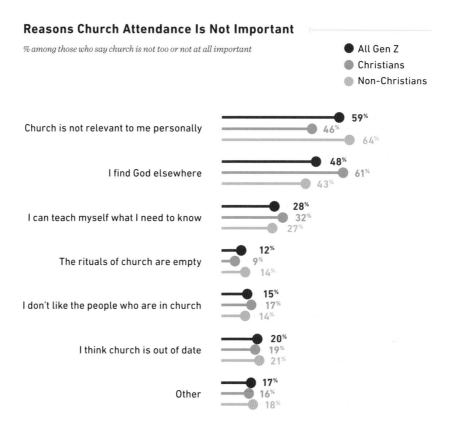

% among those who say church is not too or not at all important

● All Gen Z
● Christians
● Non-Christians

Church is not relevant to me personally
59%
46%
64%

I find God elsewhere
48%
61%
43%

I can teach myself what I need to know
28%
32%
27%

The rituals of church are empty
12%
9%
14%

I don't like the people who are in church
15%
17%
14%

I think church is out of date
20%
19%
21%

Other
17%
16%
18%

U.S. churched teens ages 13–18, *n*=219, July 7–18, 2017.

In 2013 Barna conducted a landmark study among Millennials to find out what kind of worship spaces appeal to them. (The findings were published in *Making Space for Millennials: A Blueprint for Your Culture, Ministry, Leadership and Facilities*.) It turns out that Gen Z has a lot in common with their young-adult counterparts when it comes to their "ideal" church—but also a few differences, just to keep things interesting! Like twentysomethings, *community* (in contrast with *privacy*) is deeply important to today's teens; if anything, they are even more drawn to the idea than Millennials. *Sanctuary* (compared to *auditorium*) also appeals to them, but not to the same extent as to young adults. They are about equally likely to say *casual* (over *dignified*) but are a bit more likely than Millennials to choose *flexible* (over *authentic*). And, surprisingly, *traditional* (more than *modern*) appeals to Gen Z, and they are a bit less enamored of *quiet* (over *loud*) than twentysomethings, to whom quiet is very important.

The "Ideal" Church: Gen Z vs. Millennials

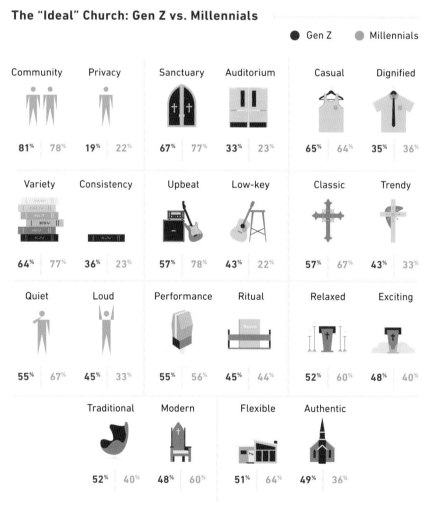

● Gen Z   ● Millennials

Community	Privacy	Sanctuary	Auditorium	Casual	Dignified
81% 78%	19% 22%	67% 77%	33% 23%	65% 64%	35% 36%

Variety	Consistency	Upbeat	Low-key	Classic	Trendy
64% 77%	36% 23%	57% 78%	43% 22%	57% 67%	43% 33%

Quiet	Loud	Performance	Ritual	Relaxed	Exciting
55% 67%	45% 33%	55% 56%	45% 44%	52% 60%	48% 40%

Traditional	Modern	Flexible	Authentic
52% 40%	48% 60%	51% 64%	49% 36%

U.S. teens ages 13–18, *n*=1,490, Nov. 4–16, 2016. U.S. adults 18–29, *n*=843, Oct. 2013.

Like Millennials (and other adult generations), Gen Z expects to see something of themselves when they walk into a church. While they appear collectively to have less intense spiritual aspirations than the age cohort immediately ahead of them, those who connect with a faith community want to know they belong.

Which brings us back around to the issue of racial and ethnic diversity. As we saw in chapters 1 and 2, Gen Z is the most diverse generation in American history—and most churches, by and large, are not. But that's not the only problem: There is also a notable lack of faith engagement among Hispanic and Asian Christians in both teens and adults. Hispanics / Latinos make up more than 13 percent of the total U.S. population but represent only 7 percent of engaged Christians among teens and 10 percent among adults. (One reason is that Catholics are less likely than Protestants to qualify as engaged, and Hispanics are disproportionately Catholic.) Similarly, Asians are nearly 6 percent of the overall population but 3 percent or less of engaged Christians.

Imagine that an unchurched or non-Christian teen or young adult visits a local church for the first time. The church is overwhelmingly white. Even if she is also white, it's conceivable she will not feel at home there because the faith community does not reflect the multicultural world she most likely lives in.

American churches' overall lack of racial and ethnic diversity could become a major stumbling block for a generation that has already begun to see church as irrelevant to their lives.

Most churches' lack of diversity could become a major stumbling block for this generation

———————————————————— z ————————————————————

Irrelevance is a key word for this generation when it comes to faith, truth and church. Not only does Christianity stand in direct contrast with many of the beliefs and attitudes of Gen Z—on the existence of objective morality and spiritual truth, for example—but the practice of the faith, especially as part of a Christian faith community, seems to many teens simply not to be relevant. It doesn't seem to have a bearing on their real day-to-day lives.

Clearly this is a challenge for those who care about making disciples in the next generation: How can you get people to pay attention to something that feels extraneous or nonsensical to their everyday lives? How do you talk about truth in a way that "feels" true?

WHERE & WHEN ARE WE LOSING YOUNG MEN?

While young men and women tend to report equal attendance at youth group, Bible studies and church during their teens years, and fall into Christian faith segments relatively equally, historic tracking shows that adult men are significantly less likely to practice Christianity (by going to church and saying their faith is important to them) than women. Is there something churches are doing, or not doing, that might explain this phenomenon? Can we stem the tide of de-churched men in our culture?

It's possible that engaging them in demanding conversation about tough topics, such as theology and morality, could make a difference. Here's why.

Gen Z males are somewhat more likely to feel they need factual evidence to support their beliefs (51% vs. 41% Gen Z girls). Additionally, young men are more likely to perceive conflict between science and the Bible (47% vs. 34%), while young women are more likely to consider science and the Bible complementary or independent (66% vs. 53% Gen Z boys). Among non-Christian teens, males are more likely than females to doubt the evidence for Christianity, with about one-quarter saying their main objection to Christianity is "I don't believe in fairy tales" (vs. 14% non-Christian Gen Z girls).

Except for a few notable exceptions, the theological beliefs of teen boys and girls are similar. But slightly fewer young men than women believe in salvation by faith in Jesus: "When you die you will go to heaven because you have confessed your sins and have accepted Jesus Christ as your savior" (29% vs. 36%). And fewer have an orthodox view of God: "God is the all-powerful, all-knowing, perfect creator of the universe who rules the world today" (47% vs. 55%).

Young men are a bit more likely to say religious people are too judgmental (20% strongly agree, 33% agree somewhat vs. 13% strongly agree, 44% agree somewhat among Gen Z girls). Some may feel this way because they harshly judge themselves: Self-identified Christian young men are more likely to feel distanced from God when they err. Three in 10 feel "like God loves you less when you do something wrong, selfish or hurtful to others," (31%) compared with one in five young Christian women (19%).

When it comes to moral questions, teen

boys are less likely than girls to say lying (32% vs. 37%) or cheating on a spouse (66% vs. 80%) is wrong.

What do we get when we add up all these data points? At least for some young men (and likely a few young women), the Christianity they know as teens is not rigorous enough to bother with as they get older; in addition to providing comfort, faith worth living must be a challenge. Many need to discover for themselves that God's love for them has no limits and that a biblical worldview can stand up to tough scrutiny.

What are we doing to strengthen young people's grit, courage and resilient faithfulness? What are we doing to challenge young men to do the hard things that following Jesus requires?

(In)Secure Orthodoxy

When it comes to statements of basic Christian orthodoxy, belief is not as strong in younger generations. Teens who believe in the historicity and divinity of Jesus, in his uniqueness as the only way to God and in the accuracy of the Bible's teachings are less likely than adults to say they are very convinced of their beliefs. For example, churchgoing teens are just as likely as churched adults to believe Jesus is the Son of God—but those who do are not as confident as adults who share the same belief. The notable exception to the rule is engaged Christians: In Gen Z and in older generations, engaged Christians share robust orthodoxy, in addition to their deep faith commitments.

- ● All Gen Z
- ● Churched teens
- ● Engaged Christian teens

- ● All adults
- ● Churched adults
- ● Engaged Christian adults

Gen Z Still (Mostly) Holds Traditional Christian Beliefs

While Gen Z is less likely than older generations to claim these beliefs, they are still more likely than not to generally agree with Christian teachings about God and Jesus (but less so about the Bible).

❝ Jesus was a real person who was crucified by Rome and was actually physically raised from the dead. *% yes*

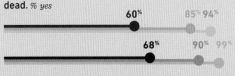

60% 85% 94%
68% 90% 99%

❝ Faith in Jesus is the only way to God. *% yes*

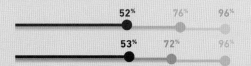

52% 76% 96%
53% 72% 96%

❝ Jesus is the divine Son of God. *% yes*

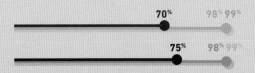

70% 98% 99%
75% 98% 99%

❝ The Bible is totally accurate in all of the principles it teaches. *% total agree*

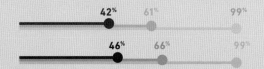

42% 61% 99%
46% 66% 99%

But Just How Sure Are They?

The real revelation comes when we follow up and ask how convinced they are of their beliefs. While most may confess the traditional teachings, Gen Z are less likely than older generations to say they are confident in their convictions. In other words, they have their doubts.

❝ Jesus was a real person who was crucified by Rome and was actually physically raised from the dead. *% very convinced*

60%
66%

❝ Faith in Jesus is the only way to God.
% very convinced

62%
74%

Teens ages 13–18, *n*=1,490, Nov. 4–16, 2016. U.S. adults ages 19 and older, *n*=1,517, Nov. 4–16, 2016.

66 **Jesus is the divine Son of God.** *% very convinced*

58%

68%

66 **The Bible is totally accurate in all of the principles it teaches.** *% strongly agree*

25%

26%

Doubt in the Church

While church involvement does make some difference, even faithful Gen Z attenders harbor significant uncertainties about their beliefs. Churched teens are not as likely as churched adults to say they are very convinced.

66 **Jesus was a real person who was crucified by Rome and was actually physically raised from the dead.** *% very convinced*

63%

72%

66 **Faith in Jesus is the only way to God.**
% very convinced

63%

77%

66 **Jesus is the divine Son of God.** *% very convinced*

63%

75%

66 **The Bible is totally accurate in all of the principles it teaches.** *% strongly agree*

31%

30%

A Bright Spot: Engaged Christians

Gen Z teens who are actively engaged in their faith express little doubt about the teachings of historical Christianity. They are just as likely as engaged Christian adults to be very convinced in their beliefs.

66 **Jesus was a real person who was crucified by Rome and was actually physically raised from the dead.** *% very convinced*

95%

99%

66 **Faith in Jesus is the only way to God.**
% very convinced

93%

93%

66 **Jesus is the divine Son of God.** *% very convinced*

99%

99%

66 **The Bible is totally accurate in all of the principles it teaches.** *% strongly agree*

87%

92%

 AT A GLANCE

Four out of five engaged Christian teens agree "I can share my honest questions, struggles and doubts with my parents" (79%),

far more than any other faith segment.

Only two out of five engaged Christian parents have ever talked to their teen about healthy media use (41%).

One-quarter reports they feel unprepared to have that conversation (24%).

Half of Protestant youth pastors say technology / social media (52%) and moral relativism (46%) are the defining factors of Gen Z.

One-quarter also points to a consumerist mindset as a defining trait (28%).

Two-thirds of youth pastors say their biggest struggle is parents who don't prioritize their teen's spiritual growth (68%).

One-third says "undoing" what the world teaches teens is their biggest struggle (33%).

Making Gen Z Disciples

Fewer U.S. teens than adults believe core theological tenets of the Christian faith—and teens who do make orthodox faith claims are not quite as sure about them as adults. Christianity, as we've already seen in teens' religious identification, has less of a hold on Gen Z than on previous generations.

Yet when researchers look at engaged Christians, a different picture emerges—not only of robust orthodoxy (that's a part of the definition of "engaged Christian," after all) but also of confident conviction. Across the board, engaged Christian teens are just as likely as their older counterparts to say they are very convinced of their Christian convictions.

This is not the case, however, for churchgoing teens who do not qualify as engaged. Churched teens are not only less confident in their beliefs than engaged teens; they are also less confident than adults in their same faith segment: churched Christians. This strongly suggests that church attendance alone is not enough for Gen Z Christians to effectively counter the prevailing post-Christian narrative that is ascendant in the broader culture.

> Church attendance alone is not enough to counter the prevailing post-Christian narrative

One difference between engaged Christian and churched teens is church activities beyond worship services. Three-quarters of engaged Christians say they regularly attend a church youth group (76%), compared to less than half of churched teens (47%); two-thirds say they are part of a regular Bible study or small group (66%), compared to just 40 percent of churchgoing youth. Some churched teens may be reluctant to attend because they are less likely than engaged Christians to agree that "My church / youth group talks intelligently about the questions that are important to me" (43% vs. 72%).

Whether or not youth groups are a factor, churched (and to a much greater extent, unchurched) Christian teens are becoming less Christian. They are becoming, as Kenda Creasy Dean calls them in her book *Almost Christian*,[28] "moralistic therapeutic deists," whose tenets are:

▸ A god exists who created and orders the world and watches over life on earth.
▸ God wants people to be good, nice and fair to each other, as taught in the Bible and by most world religions.

- ▸ The central goal of life is to be happy and to feel good about oneself.
- ▸ God is not involved in my life except when I need God to resolve a problem.
- ▸ Good people go to heaven when they die.

If the goal is to impart a vibrant, lasting faith to the next generation, this is not a promising state of affairs. Because we know the vast majority of people who have a biblical worldview in adulthood formed their values and assumptions before the age of 20 (and most before 13), now is the time to assess discipleship priorities and methods—and adjust as necessary.[29]

In the interest of assessing current priorities and methods—and to get their up-close views of today's teens—Barna surveyed engaged Christian parents of Gen Z and church youth pastors. Let's start with what parents have to say.

Engaged Christian Parents

It is very important to engaged Christian parents that their child develops a lasting faith. More than nine out of 10 also say it is important that their child "is equipped to explain the Christian faith" and is "engaged in service"—likely as elements of the overall goal of strong adult faith.

In response to an open-ended question about their hopes and dreams for their child, one-third of these parents cite "living a life of faith" above other priorities like "successful career" (24%) or "being a good person" (17%). Similarly, "remaining faithful in a secular culture" is the top fear or concern of engaged Christian parents with regard to their teen, with 28 percent describing such a scenario. One in five may have something similar in mind when they point to a "hostile society" as their greatest concern (22%).

Who owns the responsibility to develop their teen's faith? According to engaged Christian parents, they do. Three out of five say that they, the parents, are primarily responsible (59%) and more than one-third that it's mostly them, with the help of church leaders (36%). They do so in a variety of ways, most often attending church and praying together.

Four out of five engaged Christian teens agree "I can share my honest questions, struggles and doubts with my parents" (79%), far more than any other faith segment. That's great! According to a majority of parents, these conversations include Christian perspectives on current events and biblical

4 out of 5 engaged Christian teens agree "I can share my honest questions, struggles and doubts with my parents"

How Important Is It to You That Your Teen…?

% among engaged Christian parents

● Very important
● Somewhat important

Develops a faith that lasts into their adulthood — 82% / 15%

Is equipped to explain the Christian faith — 63% / 29%

Engages in service — 57% / 36%

Has a consistent quiet time — 47% / 40%

Is able to integrate their faith into their vocation or career — 43% / 36%

Attends a Christian college — 15% / 27%

Regular Family Activities

% among engaged Christian parents

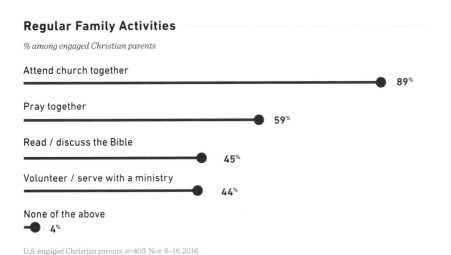

Attend church together — 89%

Pray together — 59%

Read / discuss the Bible — 45%

Volunteer / serve with a ministry — 44%

None of the above — 4%

U.S. engaged Christian parents, *n*=403, Nov. 8–16, 2016.

perspectives on sexuality and marriage. Fewer than half, however, have ever discussed (among other topics) healthy media consumption or the relationship between science and the Bible—two subjects certainly at daily issue in their teens' lives. Additionally, less than one-quarter of engaged parents have talked about integrating faith and career; even fewer have talked with their teen about discerning God's will in their choice of college. These are areas of utmost concern to many teenagers, especially older teens who are thinking deeply about planning for their future. Understanding how their plans fit with God's purpose is a big part of keeping a faith that lasts.

But parents, like their engaged Christian teens, don't all feel comfortable having conversations about difficult topics. Fewer than half report there is no topic about which they feel unprepared to talk with their teen. Surprisingly, one in five says they do not feel prepared to address "tough" questions about Christianity, God or the Bible. One in seven feels unprepared to talk about the foundational beliefs of Christianity. And about the same number struggles to

Topics Parents Have Discussed with Teens

% among engaged Christian parents

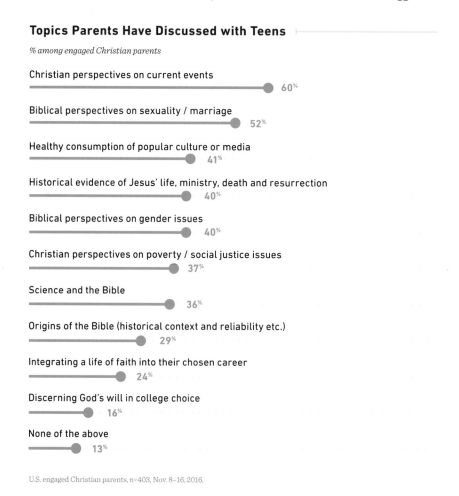

Christian perspectives on current events
60%

Biblical perspectives on sexuality / marriage
52%

Healthy consumption of popular culture or media
41%

Historical evidence of Jesus' life, ministry, death and resurrection
40%

Biblical perspectives on gender issues
40%

Christian perspectives on poverty / social justice issues
37%

Science and the Bible
36%

Origins of the Bible (historical context and reliability etc.)
29%

Integrating a life of faith into their chosen career
24%

Discerning God's will in college choice
16%

None of the above
13%

U.S. engaged Christian parents, *n*=403, Nov. 8–16, 2016.

Topics Parents Feel Unprepared to Discuss with Teens

% among engaged Christian parents

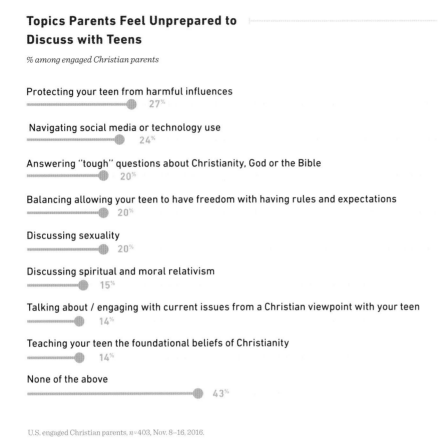

Protecting your teen from harmful influences
27%

Navigating social media or technology use
24%

Answering "tough" questions about Christianity, God or the Bible
20%

Balancing allowing your teen to have freedom with having rules and expectations
20%

Discussing sexuality
20%

Discussing spiritual and moral relativism
15%

Talking about / engaging with current issues from a Christian viewpoint with your teen
14%

Teaching your teen the foundational beliefs of Christianity
14%

None of the above
43%

U.S. engaged Christian parents, *n*=403, Nov. 8–16, 2016.

address spiritual and moral relativism—which, as we've seen, is a potent challenge to Gen Z faith.

Three-quarters of engaged Christian parents say their teen attends a youth program at church at least once a month (74%); two-thirds report they attend weekly or more often (65%). According to parents whose teens attend monthly, the programs have a few strengths in common. Worship and positive peer relationships rank at the top, with "providing a place for teens to ask serious questions about the Bible or foundational Christian beliefs" at the bottom of the list. (See p. 86.)

Unfortunately, some youth programs also appear to have a few weaknesses in common, according to parents.

Do youth pastors, the leaders of those programs, agree?

Strengths of Church's Youth Program

% among engaged Christian parents whose teen attends youth group

Providing a place for teens to worship together
42%

Creating a place for your teen to develop positive peer relationships
34%

Providing opportunities for your teen to serve or volunteer
28%

Helping teens understand the reasons and evidence for why Christianity is true
27%

Providing a place for teens to ask serious questions about the Bible or foundational Christian beliefs
23%

Weaknesses of Church's Youth Program

% among engaged Christian parents whose teen attends youth group

Helping teens determine their career / vocation
34%

Equipping teens to talk about their faith with people who do not share their beliefs
16%

Facilitating a consistent small group / Bible study for your teen
14%

Helping teens to develop personal devotional habits
14%

Providing mentorship relationships with Christian adults
14%

U.S. engaged Christian parents, *n*=299, Nov. 8–16, 2016.

Youth Pastors

Youth pastors' perceptions of Gen Z overall are a window into their experience pastoring diverse groups of students. They are well aware of the cultural challenges unique to today's teens, particularly in the areas of media consumption and moral relativism.

Just over half of youth pastors mention the impact of social media and technology on the way this generation thinks and on their capacity to interact

Most Defining Factors of Gen Z, According to Youth Pastors

% among Protestant youth pastors

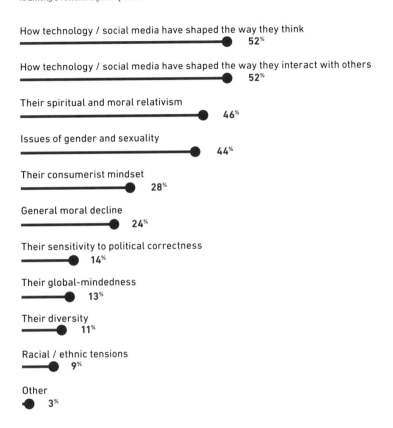

How technology / social media have shaped the way they think
52%

How technology / social media have shaped the way they interact with others
52%

Their spiritual and moral relativism
46%

Issues of gender and sexuality
44%

Their consumerist mindset
28%

General moral decline
24%

Their sensitivity to political correctness
14%

Their global-mindedness
13%

Their diversity
11%

Racial / ethnic tensions
9%

Other
3%

U.S. Protestant youth pastors, *n*=335, Nov. 16, 2016– Jan. 17, 2017; respondents could select three.

with others. And, indeed, we saw in chapter 1 how social media has captivated today's teens and influences their worldview more than ever before. The next most common answer is spiritual and moral relativism and, as we saw in chapter 2, Gen Z has the most relativistic perspective yet on truth and morality.

Youth pastors' assessments are spot-on. These are defining factors for Gen Z.

But these factors have greater and lesser impact on teens' lives for a variety of reasons—most powerfully, their parents' faith engagement, or lack thereof.

In large measure, engaged Christian parents and youth pastors are talking about two different groups of kids. The reality is that youth groups

Youth Pastors' Biggest Struggles in Ministry

% among Protestant youth pastors

Parents not prioritizing their teen's spiritual growth
68%

Lack of consistent participation
45%

"Undoing" what the world teaches them
33%

Balancing the needs of unchurched teens with growing those who do have a faith
27%

Having to entertain teens to keep them coming back
22%

Parents not aligned with beliefs and practices I am trying to instill
21%

Having the time to really get to know the teens in my ministry
16%

Getting teens to talk about the "hard" or "complex" questions about beliefs, worldview and / or morality
12%

No time to really "go deep" on topics that matter
10%

Students are unwilling to "go deep" on topics that matter
10%

Too much time dealing with practical life topics and not enough time talking about foundational beliefs
9%

Being ill-equipped, myself, to answer "hard" or "complex" questions about beliefs, worldview and / or morality
3%

Other
2%

U.S. Protestant youth pastors, *n*=335, Nov. 16, 2016–Jan. 17, 2017.

serve teens with a range of spiritual maturity levels—non-Christians to engaged Christians, and everyone in between—so by necessity leaders do not generally communicate at a spiritually or biblically sophisticated level. This is an important strategy for coaching new believers, but not so much for a teen whose parents regularly read the Bible and discuss matters of faith at home with her. It's therefore understandable why some engaged Christian parents perceive their teen's youth group as weak in some discipleship-focused areas.

We can see the tough spot youth pastors are often in by looking at their most common struggles: The top contender by far is "parents not prioritizing their teen's spiritual growth." By and large, youth pastors are not talking about engaged Christian parents! Nearly three in 10 admit that "balancing the needs of unchurched teens with growing those who do have faith" is a struggle, and one in 11 says "too much time dealing with practical life topics and not enough time talking about foundational beliefs" is a problem for their group. So at least some youth pastors are aware that the youth program is not ideal for in-depth discipleship with teens who already have a faith-engaged family.

When we look at the topics youth pastors have covered during the past year, it's clear that most are trying to plant seeds of ideas and habits in teens that will grow into mature faith. This is in line with their stated priorities, which focus on basic theology, Bible literacy and devotional habits.

▶ Prayer / devotional habits
▶ Basic theology
▶ How to read / study the Bible
▶ Sexuality, dating and marriage
▶ Origins, history, reliability of the Bible

Comparing youth pastors' discussion topics with engaged Christian parents' (see p. 84), it becomes clear that youth pastors are more likely to have talked with teens about most subjects on the list. This is partly due to the nature of their different roles: It is literally a youth pastor's job to talk about these things.

That being the case, how prepared do they feel? Nearly all think they are at least somewhat prepared for each of the four specific worldview topics addressed at length in the survey—but more are very comfortable talking about the evidence for Jesus and the origins of the Bible than about science

> Youth groups serve teens with a range of spiritual maturity levels— non-Christians to engaged Christians, and everyone in between

All youth pastors and Christian parents need to prepare for robust conversations on four worldview topics

and dialog with people of different faiths and backgrounds. (These four topics were chosen because each of them is perennially significant for Christians in any generation and of particular importance for Gen Z, given the cultural challenges they face.)

Considering the climate in which Gen Z is coming of age, all youth pastors (and Christian parents) need to prepare for robust conversations on these and other topics relating to biblical worldview. Teens may not be entirely at ease talking about these subjects, but that doesn't make them any less urgent.

How Prepared Youth Pastors Feel to Discuss Four Worldview Topics

% among Protestant youth pastors

● Very prepared
● Somewhat prepared

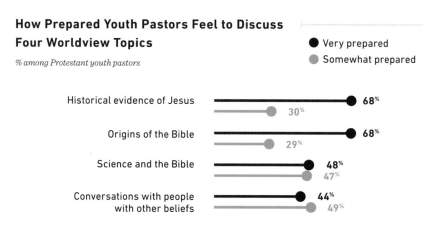

Historical evidence of Jesus — 68% / 30%
Origins of the Bible — 68% / 29%
Science and the Bible — 48% / 47%
Conversations with people with other beliefs — 44% / 49%

How Comfortable Teens Are Asking Questions About Four Worldview Topics, According to Youth Pastors

% among Protestant youth pastors

● Very comfortable
● Somewhat comfortable

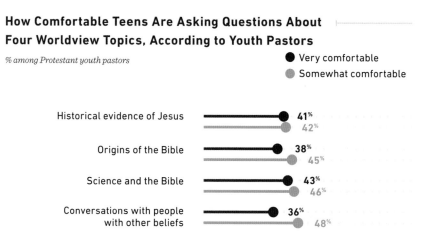

Historical evidence of Jesus — 41% / 42%
Origins of the Bible — 38% / 45%
Science and the Bible — 43% / 46%
Conversations with people with other beliefs — 36% / 48%

U.S. Protestant youth pastors, *n*=335, Nov. 16, 2016–Jan. 17, 2017.

(Continued on page 94)

Q & A WITH
JOIVAN JIMENEZ

**SINGER-SONGWRITER, ACTOR AND MINISTRY DIRECTOR
AT MEADOWBROOK CHURCH**

Joivan is a singer-songwriter and actor born in Panama City, Panama. He serves as Spanish Ministry Director and Worship Leader at Meadowbrook Church in Ocala, Florida, and worked as a student pastor for more than 15 years. Joivan is a 2017 Dove Awards nominee for his single "Generación de Fuego," nominated as Spanish Recorded Song of the Year. He enjoys cooking, watching movies and traveling with his wife, Lucianne, and their three children, Yessaira, Joilianne and Joivan Alexander. He is proud to hold both Panamanian and American citizenship, and is a voice for a comprehensive immigration reform in the United States.

You have expressed special concern about young men leaving the church and the faith as they become adults. What are some ways the Christian community can help young men stay faithful?

I was shocked when I first read about the severe drop-off in young men compared to young women, but then I thought more about it and—yeah, that's right. We are losing young men.

First, we've got to give guys opportunities to dig in and open up, to ask questions without fear of being shut down. I think gender-specific small groups should be part of the equation, to help keep focus on what matters. It's hard to show off and be real at the same time.

Second, I think sometimes male leaders are especially hard on young men because we know what it's like. We put so much pressure on them not to make mistakes, to walk perfect. And they feel guilty just for being male, for experiencing the temptations that are normal for young men their age. But they need to know God loves them. He is not condemning them. His Spirit can give them power to keep walking, even when their walk is not perfect.

Third, we've got to open more doors to ministry. When I was coming up, there was a huge push for young men to pursue a ministry calling. Ministry was exciting! We were called by God to change the world! But to us, "ministry" was "pulpit ministry"—you were only called if you were called to preach in church. But ministry is way beyond the pulpit. Kids can be called into ministry in the arts, in sports, in cooking, in science, whatever. Ministry is still exciting! But we've got to open the doors for young men (and young ladies, too) to pursue a higher calling.

z

Q & A W I T H
T R O Y E A R N E S T

AREA DIRECTOR FOR YOUNG LIFE

Troy has been on staff with Young Life for 13 years, where he oversees adults who invest in the lives of kids in Atlanta, Georgia. Under his leadership, Young Life's outreach on the eastside has increased from two schools to seven, and from 10 volunteers to 80. When he isn't running around with leaders, kids and folks in the community, Troy works on photography, listens to vinyl records and supports the Georgia Bulldogs.

I feel like some churches have seen the success of Young Life and have pivoted away from discipleship to do more outreach, similar to our approach.

I've been with youth leaders who literally ask me, "Tell me the specifics of how you do your meeting because we want to do exactly that." And I'm like, no. Don't do what we're doing. These kids need a community to go deep with, to really dig into discipleship. If churches aren't going to make that a priority, what then? Where do these kids go when they've made a commitment to Christ? In some ways, we've had to become a one-stop shop.

But then, I read the Barna data and I don't think that's ideal. Obviously there are kids who are ready to go super deep, but leaders can't cater to them—in our outreach, that would be putting truth and faith out of reach for a lot of the students. But I'm sure that's frustrating for more spiritually mature believers. We try to offer different groups based on where kids are at and that seems to help—different environments aimed at different kids.

The thing I wish youth groups would take from us is to focus on knowing kids, loving kids, showing up on their turf and befriending them. There seems to be a big focus on creating the right environment before they even get started. "We're gonna spend all this money and have this great room, and there will be video games. Kids will definitely come." But I don't think that's true. Or, if kids come to check it out, they probably won't stay.

Because they want community, not a cool environment. Build a community of people who are committed to Christ and get serious about studying the Scriptures together—and invite the kids you're going out of your way to know and love into that community.

Worldview Discipleship

We've looked throughout this report at various inputs and aspects of Gen Z's worldview: the values, allegiances and assumptions that are the (often invisible) eyeglasses through which they perceive their world. George Barna, founder of Barna Group, has long maintained that developing a biblical worldview is an essential pillar of unshakeable faith. And because that's a view shared by Barna's research partner for this study, Impact 360 Institute, researchers took a deep dive into the four biblical worldview topics introduced above. Youth pastors and engaged Christian parents were asked about teens' exposure to and views on historical evidence of Jesus, origins of the Bible, and science and the Bible. Youth pastors were also asked about having conversations with people of other or no religious faith.

Across the board, engaged Christian parents tend to perceive that their engaged Christian kids have fairly well-developed views on the topics and that, for the most part, their views are quite similar to their parents'. Youth pastors, on the other hand, say most of their students come into conversation on these topics with less-developed views, and that those views are only somewhat similar to the youth pastor's own positions.

Percentage of Teens Who Have a View on Four Worldview Topics, According to Youth Pastors and Parents

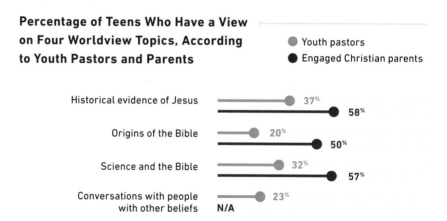

- ● Youth pastors
- ● Engaged Christian parents

Historical evidence of Jesus — 37% / 58%

Origins of the Bible — 20% / 50%

Science and the Bible — 32% / 57%

Conversations with people with other beliefs — 23% / N/A

% "majority of teens" among U.S. Protestant youth pastors, n=335, Nov. 16, 2016–Jan. 17, 2017; % "strong views" among U.S. engaged Christian parents, n=404, Nov. 8–16, 2016.

Similarity of Teens' Views to Youth Pastors' and Parents' on Four Worldview Topics

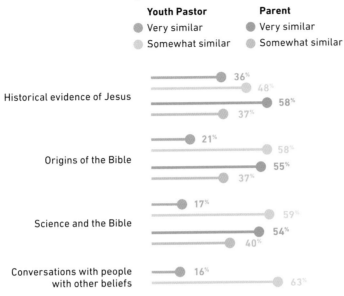

Youth Pastor
● Very similar
● Somewhat similar

Parent
● Very similar
● Somewhat similar

Historical evidence of Jesus
- 36%
- 48%
- 58%
- 37%

Origins of the Bible
- 21%
- 58%
- 55%
- 37%

Science and the Bible
- 17%
- 59%
- 54%
- 40%

Conversations with people with other beliefs
- 16%
- 63%

U.S. Protestant youth pastors, *n*=335, Nov. 16, 2016–Jan. 17, 2017; U.S. engaged Christian parents, *n*=403, Nov. 8–16, 2016; respondents indicated teen had a point of view on the topic.

According to the engaged parents and youth pastors who have talked with teens about these worldview issues, what would they say was the outcome? How well are teens able to marshal facts, evidence and persuasive arguments in support of their views?

According to engaged Christian parents, pretty well. According to youth pastors . . . not as much.

Again, the significant disparities we see here are due, in large measure, to parents talking about a smaller subset of the whole youth group that pastors have in mind. We can see similar gaps in Christian teens' self-reported confidence in their ability to support their views on a different topic: the existence of God. Engaged Christians feel much more confident than churched and unchurched teens. (See p. 96.)

Engaged Christian teens are more confident than other Christians, according to parents, youth pastors and teens themselves

Teen Confidence in Supporting Their Views on Three Worldview Topics, According to Parents & Youth Pastors

% among engaged Christian parents and Protestant youth pastors

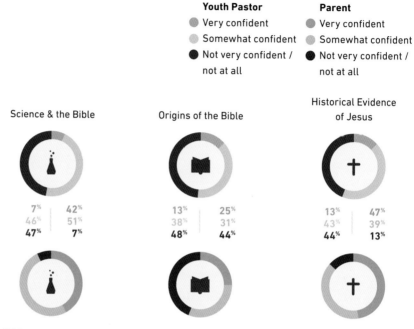

Youth Pastor
- Very confident
- Somewhat confident
- Not very confident / not at all

Parent
- Very confident
- Somewhat confident
- Not very confident / not at all

Science & the Bible

7%   42%
46% 51%
47% 7%

Origins of the Bible

13% 25%
38% 31%
48% 44%

Historical Evidence of Jesus

13% 47%
43% 39%
44% 13%

U.S. Protestant youth pastors, *n*=335, Nov. 16, 2016–Jan. 17, 2017; U.S. engaged Christian parents, *n*=404, Nov. 8–16, 2016.

Teen Confidence in the Existence of God, According to Teens

- Very confident
- Somewhat confident
- Not very confident / not at all

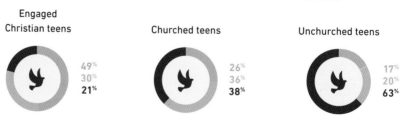

Engaged Christian teens

49%
30%
21%

Churched teens

26%
36%
38%

Unchurched teens

17%
20%
63%

U.S. teens ages 13–18, *n*=869 Nov. 4–16, 2016.

What can we take away from these assessments by parents and pastors?

Analysts believe these data are strong indicators that worldview discipleship is absolutely essential for lasting faith. To return to the metaphor of "digital Babylon" introduced by David Kinnaman early on in this report, the kids whose parents are consciously, intentionally training their minds and hearts in the ways of Jerusalem are much better prepared than "culturally Christian" teens to thrive in Babylon as the people of God. Youth pastors' unique vantage point gives us a bird's-eye view of moralistic therapeutic deism's inescapability in Gen Z—even and especially in those who merely identify as Christian. They simply are not confident enough in Christian orthodoxy . . . yet.

> Worldview discipleship is absolutely essential for lasting faith

Q & A WITH
JONATHAN MORROW

DIRECTOR OF CULTURAL ENGAGEMENT AT IMPACT 360 INSTITUTE

Jonathan has been equipping students and parents in biblical worldview, apologetics and culture for 15 years, and is passionate about seeing a new generation build a lasting faith. He holds a Master of Divinity, Master in Philosophy of Religion and Ethics, and a Doctorate in Worldview and Culture from Talbot School of Theology. He is the director of cultural engagement at Impact 360 Institute (Impact360.org) and an adjunct professor of apologetics at Biola University. He is author of several books, including *Welcome to College*, and contributed to the *Apologetics Study Bible for Students*. Jonathan and his wife have been married for 16 years and live with their three children near Atlanta.

Many teens appear hesitant to hold firm beliefs on moral or religious issues. Why do you think that is? What are the cultural factors that make it hard for them to discuss or make moral and religious claims?

I think there are two main reasons. First is the fear of being perceived as judgmental, unloving or intolerant. Our natural desire to be liked by others and our aversion to conflict notwithstanding, Christians genuinely don't want to come across as judgmental.

The problem here is that teenagers are confusing making a judgment about a question that matters with being judgmental. This confusion flows from a misunderstanding of Jesus' command not to judge in Matthew 7:1–6. But a closer look at the context reveals that Jesus is for making judgments between good and evil, between what is morally right and wrong, between what is true and what is false. What he is completely against is people using knowledge of the truth to beat others up and belittle them, or to make themselves appear morally superior. Self-righteousness is not a Christian virtue.

Moreover, tolerance is not agreement—it is extending to others the right to be wrong and treating them with dignity and respect. And in terms of being loving, sometimes the most loving thing you can do is tell someone the truth. Loving our neighbor well means seeking their highest good in word and deed.

Another reason students are hesitant to hold firm on moral or spiritual truth is what

I will call the crisis of knowledge. Knowledge is what authorizes and enables us to navigate reality. Knowledge is what I want my mechanic and dentist to have before I let them do anything to my car or to me. But our culture no longer assumes that spiritual and moral knowledge are a possibility—there is only opinion, personal preference and blind faith.

Why is this? Because we have inherited a way of viewing the world that believes only the hard sciences give us knowledge. In other words: You can't know something unless you prove it scientifically. This view is called scientism. In Gen Z, scientism is not even argued for; it is assumed.

Yet it's obvious that we can know things outside of the hard sciences, like truths about the past (history) or that human trafficking is objectively evil (morality).

The bottom line is that the Bible assumes moral and spiritual knowledge exist (see Hos. 4:1–6; Luke 1:1–4; Romans 1:19; 2:15; 1 John 5:13). But when Christians talk about this knowledge with our culture, our culture hears it as an individual taste, not as reality. So why have an uncomfortable conversation with a friend or teammate about religion or morality if it's just like choosing a flavor of ice cream?

But if it's medicine that will cure us, that is a different story.

In light of the challenges Gen Z faces with information overload and confusion about truth, how can leaders and parents help students build a strong faith?

Culture is what people come to see as normal. We don't think about it. Whether we realize it or not, there are shaping and normalizing forces at work every second of every day in our society, schools and mobile devices. There is no way for teenagers—or any of us, for that matter—to grow up in a culture and not be shaped.

What is true and good can become normal for a generation, but so can what is false and harmful.

A person's worldview is a web of habit-forming beliefs about the biggest questions of life that helps them make sense of all their experiences. Everyone has a worldview. And as followers of Jesus, we are not to passively allow ourselves to be shaped by our culture. We are not to conform to the ways of this world, we are to be conformed to God's ways and become more like Jesus (see Rom. 8:29; 12:2).

As I have worked with Christian teenagers over the past 15 years, I have developed a framework that I call the "Three Rs of Worldview Transformation." In order to build a strong and lasting faith, students need reasons, relationships and rhythms. These are the things we can directly influence.

First teenagers need reasons for faith: to know why they believe what they believe (see 1 Pet. 3:15). Apologetics is not optional. They also need to be inoculated against false ideas while they are younger and in an environment where we can help them discover reasonable responses to objections to their faith. This requires safe space for them to ask questions and explore doubts. In short, teenagers need a grown-up worldview, not coloring-book Jesus. It's so fun to see teenagers' confidence grow and their faith come alive when they discover that Christianity is actually true!

Next, teenagers need wise relationships. Gen Z increasingly feels isolated and alone, but they hunger for real relationships. There are four strategic relationships we can help them cultivate: God, parents, mentors and friends (see Prov. 13:20). I am convinced that relationships are the most powerful shaping influence during the teenage years.

Last, students need rhythms to help them practice their faith. We become what we repeatedly do. Teenagers can't build a strong worldview if they never practice it. We must help students ask who they are becoming. Formation of virtue is more than just doing the right thing; it's about becoming the kind of person who loves what is good. Through rhythms and spiritual practices, we can indirectly affect our desires, loves and character (see Heb. 5:14). In addition to the work of God's Spirit and our response to his grace, this process takes time, intentionality, honest conversation and mentors.

One of the things we have learned by working with Gen Z at Impact 360 Institute is that you can't mass-produce transformation. True information is essential, but by itself it is not enough. It's just as essential that students have space, relationships and practices to take ownership of their faith.

As our post-Christian culture increasingly marginalizes Christianity, it is critical for those of us who care about the next generation not to take a business-as-usual approach to their formation. If we do nothing they will be shaped away from life with God in Christ. We have the opportunity to reimagine what passing on our faith to the next generation looks like in this unique cultural moment. Let's be creative, courageous and faithful!

HOPE FOR THEIR (AND OUR) FUTURE

It may go without saying, but today's teenagers are not growing up in their grandparents' or their parents' world—not even in their twentysomething cousin's world. Rapid changes in technology, communication, science, law and worldview are creating a world for teenagers that leaves many parents, church leaders and other mentors feeling flummoxed.

Of course, changes to culture are not changes to the essence of what it means to be human. Teens today, like teens of long ago, wrestle with insecurity, bullying, boredom, loneliness, raging hormones, paralyzing doubt. They navigate their first crushes, question their parents' beliefs and dream of their future. Perhaps what adults need first and foremost to remind ourselves is this: We were there once, too. *They are not so very different from us at that age.*

Yet it is foolish to believe teens—even Christian teens—are immune to the surrounding culture. Confusion about what it means to be good and do good is not confined outside of church doors or Christian homes; virtual connections fling wide the doors whether we like it or not. "How can we protect our kids?" is, therefore, not the crucial question to answer. Rather, the most urgent question for parents, pastors and teachers is, "How do we prepare them to follow Christ?"

> The most urgent question for parents, pastors and teachers is, "How do we prepare teens to follow Christ?"

In some ways Gen Z's generational ethos naturally resonates with a life of Christian faith, and in others their collective worldview clashes with the Church's traditions and beliefs. By looking squarely at both would-be clashes and resonances, those involved in making disciples among the next generation can be most effective.

Let's start with an overview of potential clashes, based on the findings of this research.

Gen Z Clashes with Christianity

TRUTH. At the most fundamental level, classic Christianity and Gen Z as a whole are deeply divided on how to know what is true (and, in some cases,

The relativism in
Gen Z is based less
on a deficit of moral
values and more on
insufficient ideas
about what truth is

on if there is such a thing as "what is true"). Christians throughout history have contended we can know God because God reveals himself in creation, in the Scriptures and, most fully, in Christ. But, as we've seen in this study, many teens express confusion and uncertainty about truth and their grasp on it. It's conceivable, even likely, that the relativism ascendant in Gen Z is based less on a general deficit of moral values and more on thin, insufficient ideas about what truth is and how to find it. More broadly, buying in to scientism and hostility toward religion doesn't so much prove the failure of Christian belief and ways of knowing, as it reveals careless, unexamined assumptions about knowledge and truth.

SEX. Relatedly, the sexual ethic embraced by so many teens and young adults is not, for most of them, a carefully considered rejection of traditional Christian ethics but blind, unthinking acceptance of *consent* as the ultimate ethical standard, which many are convinced renders any and all sexual activity morally neutral. (This is one reason porn is so ubiquitous among Gen Z and Millennials—not only because mobile technology has made it easily accessible, but also because it appears not to break the inviolable "law of consent.") Christianity insists there is an inescapable moral dimension to sexual desire and activity far beyond mere consent—and that insistence clashes with the limited "do no harm" ethic prevalent in young America today.

MONEY. Another generational value that cuts against the grain of Christian teaching is Gen Z's focus on personal happiness and financial success. There is, of course, nothing inherently wrong with having enough money to care for family and meet financial obligations. But the New Testament writers are clear that making pursuit of wealth one's primary life goal is spiritually dangerous and even destructive. Gen Z is certainly not alone in their battle to put wealth in its proper place—this is an arena where American Christianity overall has struggled to maintain its prophetic witness to a culture consumed with consuming. Perhaps walking alongside the next generation will also help older Christians rethink their own relationships with material success and personal happiness.

TECH. Parents and mentors may feel it's too late to slam shut the Pandora's box of mobile devices, yet perpetual use of technology to mediate relationships could be the biggest clash of all with a Christian way of life. From its earliest days after Pentecost, the Church has been in conversation about what it means to be the Body of Christ—and *how.* While leaders have managed to disagree on just about every other particular, the historical consensus has been notably lasting and robust when it comes to God's people gathering in unity to share in the fellowship of the Holy Spirit. (In case you're wondering, Christians should definitely set aside time to do that on a regular basis.) The Church's persistence in this practice is based on myriad theological and historical arguments, not least of which is that *physical presence matters*. The Lord was raised to new life in a physical (albeit glorified) body. He instituted the Eucharist or Communion, a physical act that nourishes human bodies, and baptism, a physical act that washes human bodies, as signs of his presence living in physical people. His apostle to the Gentiles wrote to faraway churches about longing to be physically present with them—in fact, Paul compared being physically separated from the Thessalonian Christians to being "orphaned" (see 1 Thess. 2:17).

Mobile devices and social media are fine, as far as they go, but they are no substitute for relationships IRL (that's "in real life" for those who don't speak text). Yes, caring adults should connect with teens in virtual space—Gen Z needs oversight and coaching on how to relate well with and through these technologies (and some teens may only feel comfortable asking hard questions in that "safe space"). But virtual connection cannot take the place of real, human, physical, face-to-face connection. Depressed, anxiety-ridden screenagers hiding out in their bedrooms need an escape hatch that opens into the Body of Christ.

> Virtual connection cannot take the place of real, human, physical, face-to-face connection

Gen Z Resonance with Christianity

Gen Z is not simply at odds with Christianity, however; their shared worldview resonates with Christian values and priorities in some regards. And it's just as important for pastors, parents and other leaders to celebrate and encourage (and learn from!) these resonances with the faith as it is to break up the clashes.

DIVERSITY. Teens' assumptions about the goodness of diversity, for example, naturally resonate with Christian faith and priorities. The Scriptures are clear that people of all races, ethnicities and nationalities belong in God's family (see Rev. 7:9), and Gen Z tends to be more comfortable than older generations with practicing diversity-in-unity *now*, as well as in the age to come. Perhaps they can coach older sisters and brothers to be respectfully at ease with different views, a key to turning aggressive polarization into confident pluralism. Yet the discomfort some teens feel with the everyday, nitty-gritty of diversity is also an opportunity for the Church. If God's people, sharing in his Spirit, can actually figure out how to belong together, given their real and sometimes intense differences, Christ's peace and reconciliation can be an unassailable witness to the most culturally diverse generation in American history.

EMPATHY. Perhaps because diverse views and experiences are the social norm for Gen Z, their tolerance threshold tends to be high and their appetite for antagonizing low. Older adults may perceive this as oversensitive or "politically correct," but teens' instincts resonate with the second half of the apostle Peter's guidance on how to live as exiles, citizens of God's kingdom scattered in a pagan empire. "If someone asks about your hope as a believer, always be ready to explain it. But do this in a gentle and respectful way" (1 Pet. 3:15-16). Instead of criticizing teens for majoring on "gentle and respectful," older believers might instead consider how they can help get Gen Z "ready to explain it"—and reflect on what they, the grownups, can learn about empathy from a gentle, respectful generation.

OPENNESS. While teens' overall ignorance of the Bible and a basic Christian view of the world may appear to be an unmitigated loss for the Church, there are some upsides. For example, many teens do not have spiritual baggage from bad Sunday school teachers or hypocritical Christians—which saves the arduous and painful task of unpacking hurtful experiences, having to "undo" what a previous church did to them. Likewise, most in Gen Z don't have deeply held bad theology to release before they can trust the Good Shepherd. Plus, a generation lacking confidence in what is true may be open in a profound way to a personal experience of God, much as those on the religious and cultural margins were often open to encountering Jesus during his earthly ministry.

EMPTINESS. Another way Gen Z's worldview welcomes the Church is deeply counterintuitive: Moralistic therapeutic deism, examined in chapter 4, can't save people. It can't rescue anybody from bondage to sin and fear of death. It doesn't invite anyone into the very life of God, filling them with the Holy Spirit and calling them to a life of eternal purpose. It can't even deliver on its own priorities of happiness, self-esteem and general niceness.

And that's good. The inevitable failure of moralistic therapeutic deism to bring anything resembling life everlasting or transcendent fulfillment is a welcome mat laid out for the people of God to bring the only One who can fill the emptiness.

Making Disciples for Babylon

But how can Gen Z become disciples in a post-Christian culture? Thankfully, the Church has centuries of experience communicating the gospel across religious, linguistic and cultural divides. We call it "missions." When a missionary immerses herself in a culture different from her own, she doesn't expect the people who live there to speak and act and think like people from home—in fact, she expects quite the opposite: that *she* will have to change in order to connect with people.

A similar situation confronts churches today. Will older Christians insist that the youngest generation must speak, act and think like us, long-time residents of Jerusalem? Or will we help young exiles become and remain the people of God in Babylon?

If the latter, then pastors, educators, mentors and parents will have to give up entertaining kids into the Kingdom. Pizza parties, silly games and worship nights may be attractive outreach events but they do not instill lasting faith. Disciple-making in Gen Z must, by necessity, involve formation in the basics: There is a God. Truth exists. This is how the world is. This is who we are. This is what Jesus does about it.

But Gen Z disciple-making must also actively engage a two-way dynamic: faith in light of culture; culture in light of faith. How we follow Christ is inevitably shaped by the culture in which we find ourselves. But it is at least equally true that the surrounding culture is transformed as *we* are transformed in Christ. How can mentors equip Gen Z not just with information *about* faith but also with critical thinking and experiences that deepen faith? Parents and educators, especially, are positioned to *proactively* guide growing teens to think well about living for Christ in a post-Christian culture.

The pace of cultural change may feel overwhelming, but don't be discouraged. Even the gates of hell cannot prevail against the Church—and that promise is for God's people in Generation Z, too.

> Gen Z disciple-making must actively engage a two-way dynamic: faith in light of culture and culture in light of faith

Notes

1. Common Sense Media, "The Common Sense Census: Media Use by Tweens and Teens," 2015. https://www.commonsense-media.org/sites/default/files/uploads/research/census_researchreport.pdf (accessed September 2017).

2. Marc Prensky, "Digital Natives, Digital Immigrants," *On the Horizon*, October 2001, Vol. 9, No. 5. https://www.marcprensky.com/writing/Prensky%20-%20Digital%20Natives,%20Digital%20Immigrants%20-%20Part1.pdf (accessed November 2017).

3. Jean Twenge, "Have Smartphones Destroyed a Generation?" *The Atlantic*, September 2017. https://www.theatlantic.com/magazine/archive/2017/09/has-the-smartphone-destroyed-a-generation/534198/ (accessed September 2017).

4. Matt Richtel, "Are Teenagers Replacing Drugs with Smartphones?" *The New York Times*, March 13, 2017. https://www.nytimes.com/2017/03/13/health/teenagers-drugs-smartphones.html?mcubz=0 (accessed September 2017).

5. Anthony Turner, "Generation Z: Technology and Social Interest," *Journal of Individual Psychology*, Summer 2015, Vol. 71, No. 2, pp. 103–113.

6. See, for example, Benjamin C. Storm, et. al, "Using the Internet to Access Information Inflates Future Use of the Internet to Access Other Information," *Memory*, July 2016, Vol. 25, pp. 717–723. http://www.tandfonline.com/doi/full/10.1080/09658211.2016.1210171 (accessed September 2017); Paul Barnwell, "Do Smartphones Have a Place in the Classroom?" *The Atlantic*, April 27, 2016. https://www.theatlantic.com/education/archive/2016/04/do-smartphones-have-a-place-in-the-classroom/480231/ (accessed September 2017); Richtel, "Are Teenagers Replacing Drugs with Smartphones?"

7. Common Sense Media, "The Common Sense Census: Media Use by Tweens and Teens."

8. Danah Boyd, *It's Complicated: The Social Lives of Networked Teens* (New Haven, CT: Yale University Press, 2014).

9. Twenge, "Have Smartphones Destroyed a Generation?"

10. Donna Freitas, *The Happiness Effect: How Social Media Is Driving a Generation to Appear Perfect at Any Cost* (New York: Oxford University Press, 2017).

11. Turner, "Generation Z and Social Interest."

12. James Emery White, *Meet Generation Z: Understanding and Reaching the New Post-Christian World* (Grand Rapids, MI: Baker Books, 2017), p. 11.

13. White, *Meet Generation Z*, p. 32.

14. Alan Levinovitz, "How Trigger Warnings Silence Religious Students," *The Atlantic*, Aug. 30, 2016. https://www.theatlantic.com/politics/archive/2016/08/silencing-religious-students-on-campus/497951/ (accessed September 2017).

15. David Kinnaman and Gabe Lyons, *Good Faith: How to Be a Christian When Society Thinks You're Irrelevant and Extreme* (Grand Rapids, MI: Baker Books, 2016).

16. Turner, "Generation Z and Social Interest."

17. Ryan Scott, "Get Ready for Generation Z," *Forbes*, Nov. 28, 2016. https://www.forbes.com/sites/causeintegration/2016/11/28/get-ready-for-generation-z/#4cfd09ae2204 (accessed September 2017).

18. Jon Brooks, "A New Generation Overthrows Gender," NPR, May 2, 2017. http://www.npr.org/sections/health-shots/2017/05/02/526067768/a-new-generation-overthrows-gender (accessed September 2017).

19. Jon Marcus, "Why Men Are the New College Minority," *The Atlantic*, Aug. 8, 2017. https://www.theatlantic.com/education/archive/2017/08/why-men-are-the-new-college-minority/536103/ (accessed September 2017).

20. White, *Meet Generation Z*, p. 39.

21. Libby Kane, "Meet Generation Z, the 'Millennials on Steroids' Who Could Lead the Charge for Change in the US," *Business Insider*, September 15, 2017. http://www.businessinsider.com/generation-z-profile-2017-9/#technology-has-shaped-their-daily-lives-and-their-worldview-1 (accessed November 2017).

22. Hanna Rosin, "The Overprotected Kid," *The Atlantic Monthly*, April 2014. https://www.theatlantic.com/magazine/archive/2014/04/hey-parents-leave-those-kids-alone/358631/ (accessed September 2017).

23. Julie Lythcott-Haims, "Kids of Helicopter Parents Are Sputtering Out," Slate.com, July 5, 2015. http://www.slate.com/articles/double_x/doublex/2015/07/helicopter_parenting_is_increasingly_correlated_with_college_age_depression.html (accessed September 2017).

24. White, *Meet Generation Z*, pp. 51–58.

25. United States Department of Labor Bureau of Labor Statistics, "Unemployment Rates by Age, Sex, and Marital Status, Seasonally Adjusted," September 2017. https://www.bls.gov/web/empsit/cpseea10.htm (accessed October 2017).

26. Twenge, "Have Smartphones Destroyed a Generation?"

27. Freitas, *The Happiness Effect*, p. 80.

28. Kenda Creasy Dean, *Almost Christian: What the Faith of Our Teenagers Is Telling the American Church* (New York: Oxford University Press, 2010).

29. See George Barna, *Transforming Children into Spiritual Champions* (Grand Rapids, MI: Baker Books, 2003, 1st ed.).

Methodology

Field Studies (Qualitative)

Barna conducted a total of four focus groups in August 2016 with U.S. teenagers between the ages of 14 and 17. Two focus groups were conducted in Atlanta, Georgia, on August 11, and two sessions were conducted in Los Angeles, California, on August 17.

The first focus group conducted in both locations consisted entirely of teenagers whose parents consider their child a Christian—either Protestant or Catholic ("Christian Group"). The second focus group conducted in both locations consisted entirely of teenagers whose parents do not consider their child a Christian ("Non-Christian Group"). The goal for all four groups was to get a sense of their priorities for life and perspectives on faith, to inform design of the quantitative survey instruments.

Nationally Representative Surveys (Quantitative)

Two nationally representative studies of teens were conducted. The first was conducted using an online consumer panel November 4–16, 2016, and included 1,490 U.S. teenagers 13 to 18 years old. The second was conducted July 7–18, 2017, and also used an online consumer panel, which included 507 U.S. teenagers 13 to 18 years old. The data from both surveys were minimally weighted to known U.S. Census data in order to be representative of ethnicity, gender, age and region.

Three hundred thirty-five U.S. Protestant youth pastors were also interviewed. Members of Barna's pastor panel who identify as the person who has direct responsibility for the church's ministry to middle- or high-school students were invited to participate in an online survey, conducted November 16, 2016–January 17, 2017.

Four hundred and three engaged Christian parents were also surveyed. To qualify for participation, parents had to 1) identify as Christian, 2) be the parent of a child ages 13 to 19, 3) have attended a church service in the past month and 4) qualify as an "engaged Christian" under the definition designed for this study (see below). The survey was conducted using an online consumer panel November 8–16, 2016.

One nationally representative study of 1,517 U.S. adults ages 19 and older was conducted using an online panel November 4–16, 2016. The data were minimally weighted to known U.S. Census data in order to be representative of ethnicity, gender, age and region.

Definitions

NO FAITH identify as agnostic, atheist or "none of the above."

OTHER FAITH identify with a religion other than Christianity.

UNCHURCHED CHRISTIANS identify as Christian but have not attended church within the past six months.

CHURCHED CHRISTIANS identify as Christian and have attended church within the past six months, but do not qualify as engaged under the definition below.

ENGAGED CHRISTIANS identify as Christian, have attended church within the past six months and strongly agree with the each of the following:

- ▸ The Bible is the inspired word of God and contains truth about the world.
- ▸ I have made a personal commitment to Jesus Christ that is still important in my life today.
- ▸ I engage with my church in more ways than just attending services.
- ▸ I believe that Jesus Christ was crucified and raised from the dead to conquer sin and death.

GEN Z were born 1999 to 2015. (Only teens 13 to 18 are included in this study.)
MILLENNIALS were born 1984 to 1998.
GEN X were born 1965 to 1983.
BOOMERS were born 1946 to 1964.
ELDERS were born before 1946.

The **BIBLICAL WORLDVIEW** definition includes the following factors:

▸ Has made a personal commitment to Jesus that is still important in their life today

▸ Believes they will go to heaven when they die "because you have confessed your sins and accepted Jesus Christ as your savior"

▸ Strongly agrees the Bible is totally accurate in all of its teachings

▸ Strongly agrees they personally have a responsibility to tell other people your religious beliefs

▸ Strongly disagrees that Jesus Christ committed sins when he lived on earth

▸ Strongly disagrees that the devil, or Satan, is not a living being but a symbol of evil

▸ Strongly disagrees that a person can earn a place in heaven if they are generally good or they do enough good things for others

▸ Believes God is the all-powerful, all-knowing, perfect creator of the universe who rules the world today

Acknowledgements

Barna Group is grateful to Jonathan Morrow for his wholehearted commitment to the next generation, and for his informed, from-the-trenches view of the findings. It has been an honor to collaborate with you and Impact 360 Institute on this gift to the Church and our next generation.

We are also deeply grateful to the scholars and practitioners who contributed insights to the *Gen Z* report: Irene Cho, Troy Earnest, Donna Freitas, Joivan Jimenez, John A. Murray and Fikre Prince.

This research would not have been possible without George Barna's pioneering work on biblical worldview. We are indebted to him and are thankful every day for what he began more than 30 years ago.

The research team for *Gen Z* is Brooke Hempell, Traci Hochmuth, Elise Miller and Pam Jacob. Under the editorial direction of Roxanne Stone, Brooke Hempell, Aly Hawkins and David Kinnaman analyzed the data and wrote this report. Alyce Youngblood developed the data visualizations, which were designed, along with the report, by Annette Allen. Doug Brown proofread the manuscript. Brenda Usery managed production with help from Todd White.

The research team wishes to thank our Barna colleagues Amy Brands, Matt Carobini, Joyce Chiu, Inga Dahlstedt, Bill Denzel, Elaine Klautzsch, Cory Maxwell-Coghlan, Steve McBeth, Susan Mettes, Josh Pearce, Lisa Schoke, Caitlin Schuman and Sara Tandon.

About the Project Partners

BARNA GROUP is a research firm dedicated to providing actionable insights on faith and culture, with a particular focus on the Christian church. In its 30-year history, Barna has conducted more than one million interviews in the course of hundreds of studies, and has become a go-to source for organizations that want to better understand a complex and changing world from a faith perspective.

Barna's clients and partners include a broad range of academic institutions, churches, nonprofits and businesses, such as Alpha, the Templeton Foundation, Fuller Seminary, the Bill and Melinda Gates Foundation, Maclellan Foundation, DreamWorks Animation, Focus Features, Habitat for Humanity, The Navigators, NBC-Universal, the ONE Campaign, Paramount Pictures, the Salvation Army, Walden Media, Sony and World Vision. The firm's studies are frequently quoted by major media outlets such as *The Economist,* BBC, CNN, *USA Today,* the *Wall Street Journal,* Fox News, Huffington Post, *The New York Times* and the *Los Angeles Times.*
www.Barna.com

IMPACT 360 INSTITUTE cultivates leaders who follow Jesus through life-changing experiences that help students live out their faith with confidence. Through biblical worldview training, community-based discipleship, leadership mentoring, vocational coaching and missional opportunities, students are equipped to live as change-agents in the world.

On-campus experiences take place at the state-of-the-art campus in Pine Mountain, Georgia. Students from around the world come to Impact 360 Institute to know Jesus more deeply, be transformed in their character and live a life of Kingdom influence. This transformation takes place through a nine-month Fellows (gap year) experience for 18-20 year olds, a two–week summer Immersion into transformational apologetics and biblical worldview for high school students, and a one-week summer experience that Propels high school students into a life of Christian influence.
www.Impact360.org

Is the church losing a generation?

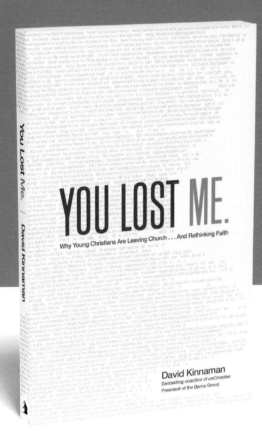

In this book, you will find:

- Research-based insights and analysis

- Contributions from experts in a variety of ministry fields

- Ideas for passing on a flourishing, deep-rooted faith

- Renewed hope in God's purpose for the next generation

Gen Z is based in part on research from *You Lost Me*, which shows that more than half of all Christian teens and twentysomethings leave active involvement in church as they transition into adulthood. The details of individual stories differ, but time and again the themes of disengagement and disconnection surface.

These spiritual shifts are a challenge to the established church, but there is still time to connect with and disciple the next generation. *You Lost Me* offers ideas for pastors, youth leaders, parents and educators to continue a legacy of vibrant faith and encourages young adults in a wholehearted pursuit of Christ.

Stay Informed About Cultural Trends

Barna Trends 2018
A beautifully designed and engaging look at today's trending topics that includes new data, analysis, infographics, and interviews right at your fingertips.

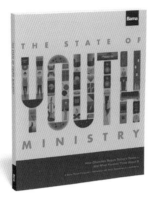

State of Youth Ministry
A wide-angle view of the youth ministry landscape that will spark conversations and lead to more effective student ministries, healthier youth workers, and sturdier teen faith.

The Porn Phenomenon
This study exposes the breadth and depth of pornography's impact and confirms that we can no longer ignore its impact on the next generation.

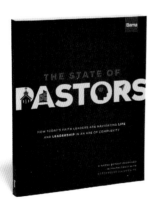

The State of Pastors
Pastoring in a complex cultural moment is not easy. Read about how church leaders are holding up in this whole-life assessment of U.S. pastors.

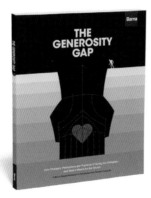

The Generosity Gap
Generosity is changing. Read about how pastors and laypeople perceive and practice generosity, and learn methods for strengthening giving habits.

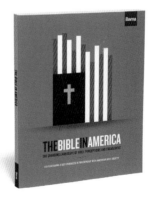

The Bible in America
Analysis, insights and encouragement for those who want to understand Scripture engagement today and how to cultivate faith that lasts in an ever-changing world.